TO BHARAT, FOR BEING
MY FOREVER HAPPY PLACE XX

# TANDOORI

## HOME COOKING

OVER 70 CLASSIC INDIAN TANDOORI
RECIPES TO COOK AT HOME

*Hardie Grant*

BOOKS

# MAUNIKA GOWARDHAN

# Introduction

When navigating your way through the bustling crowds of Khau Galli — 'Khau' meaning to eat, 'Galli' meaning street — on Mohammed Ali Road in Mumbai, go wherever the aromas of the grilled tandoori food direct you. Street carts and kebab stalls line up across the narrow alleyway and the aromas reach the end of the road. I make my way in anticipation to sample all the deliciousness — a variety of melt-in-the-mouth kebabs, tandoori tikkas, naans, chutneys and salads. As I get closer, the vendors can be heard chanting in rhythm, listing the dishes on the menu board, including all the specials that change daily. Walking up to our regular street stall, Hussain knows the order by heart. He appears with platefuls of tandoori chicken tikkas, charcoal-grilled lamb chops with ginger and chilli, charred stuffed green bell peppers, malai tikkas slathered with butter, lime and chaat masala, freshly made rotis and parathas from the specials' board some delicious green marinated haraa paneer tikka. There is also a trio of tangy fresh chutneys, some pakoras and a moreish pickled salad. Eating all of this is an explosion of flavours, yet the experience of being there is so much more than the satiating food we eat. As well as the smoky, charred flavours, it's also the enticing aromas, the crackle of the burning charcoal and the sizzle of the food on the burners, the hum of the busy street traffic, the familiar faces of the vendors, the servers and the many customers who have frequented these stalls through the years.

When we think about tandoori cooking dating back to the Indus Valley civilization, it's always about the technique of cooking in a clay oven — the rustic breads, vegetables and meat cooked in the tandoor — and ultimately about the community it fed. This came to even greater prominence through the Grand Trunk Road, which popularly ran as a life-sustaining link from Kabul in Afghanistan to Kolkata in West Bengal, a route used by traders and invaders across the centuries. During partition (the division of India and Pakistan in 1947) millions of separated families made their way along the GT Road and amidst all this chaos communal kitchens became the essential backbone for immigrants. These shared kitchens centered around the clay oven (tandoor), providing food, warmth and a safe haven, if only for a while. That glow of a tandoor became ubiquitous, providing affordable home-cooked food to comfort and nurture the soul. To this day, when we think of tandoori cooking, it resonates with all these values: a hot meal, some warmth and a sense of community are constant needs in uncertain times.

The traditional, age-old tandoor is an unfired clay vessel with walls strengthened by straw. Discoveries at Mohenjo-daro (a famous archaeological site in Pakistan) show that the tandoor originated back in 2600 B.C. The first tandoors were used to bake flatbread, a tradition that survives in Indian roti, Afghan naan and Turkmen chorek. These ancient tandoors were discovered overground as well as underground. Over time, the Mughals (the ruling dynasty within India during the 16th to 19th centuries) used this cooking technique in many of their recipes and Nawabs (who enjoyed princely status within the Mughal empire) found ways to travel with portable tandoors to ensure food cooked in the royal kitchens included tandoori tikkas, smoky kebabs and stuffed whole chickens. The traditions of tandoori cooking travelled the length of India and were taken all the way to places like the southern region of Karnataka, with cities including Hyderabad brimming with Awadhi cooking influences from the north.

Many communities subsequently drifted into food businesses, not just across north India but through varied regions, setting up tandoors within restaurants or standalone street stalls. By the 1950s, major cities including Bombay and Calcutta had become synonymous with tandoori cooking, including dishes like the famous tandoori chicken tikka, which is widely credited to Kundan Lal Gujral and its humble beginnings at his restaurant in Peshawar, Pakistan. In 1968, the *Good Food Guide* in the UK reported the Gaylord Restaurant to be the first Indian restaurant in London to be using a 'mud oven' to cook 'tandoori chicken masal' and 'nan'. Many restaurants across the UK followed their lead and installed a tandoor to be able to serve their diners tandoori dishes. A global fan following developed for this traditional cuisine and cooking technique from ancient India.

Despite its ancient origins and simplistic cooking method, the tandoor yields amazing results, from smoky, soft flatbreads to chargrilled, succulent meats. The direct high heat from the burning charcoal gives similar results to grilling or roasting the food, while keeping the heat steady. The clay walls are used to cook smoky flatbreads within minutes, which has continually been compared to traditional baking. One of the biggest advantages of these tandoor ovens is that, once they are heated, they maintain a consistent high temperature for hours with very little additional fuel. This is beneficial when fuel is scarce. The high temperature seals the flavour in the ingredients, while being a healthier method of cooking as the natural fat within the meat renders. You only then need to use minimal extra ghee or butter for basting.

Meat and vegetable tikkas cooked on skewers take on that classic tandoori flavour with their coating of marinade, which drips onto the hot coals during cooking, creating smoke. And as such, marinades for tandoori dishes are an essential vehicle for flavour. Too spicy and the meat or vegetables will be smothered by its flavour. Too bland and the ingredients will not taste of much. The consistency of the marinade is vital, too, as it needs to be thick enough to coat the chicken, lamb or vegetables without all of it dripping off or the ingredients drying out during the cooking process.

Replicating these tandoori flavours at home always reminds me of eating my way along the Mohammed Ali Road and all the regional varieties I have sampled during my travels through the varied communities of India. These food experiences are based in the local landscape, ancient traditions, culinary customs and, importantly, historic immigration through the Indian subcontinent. Living in the UK now, I have seen how barbecue cooking in the west is limited to the alfresco summer cooking season. However, with a limited British summer, I'm keen to bring these flavours indoors and replicate the smoky kebabs, tikkas, flatbreads, chutneys and salads using a conventional oven and grill so they can be enjoyed all year round. There is so much more to cooking with a grill than a classic tandoori chicken tikka! So let me take you on a tandoori cooking journey that takes in classic marinades, grilled vegetables, paneer, meats, fish and seafood, alongside fresh breads, delicious salads, fiery chutneys and tangy dressings that will show you how simple ingredients can bring together the most delicious flavours and aromas right at home.

Modern conventional ovens replicate the heat pattern of a tandoor in similar ways with a roasting and grilling setting. You might be surprised to learn that I only began cooking dishes in an oven when I moved to the UK. We never had an oven in India. For the longest time, an oven has never been part of an Indian home, as most cooking is done over a gas hob. At my home in Mumbai, tikkas were made on a frying pan (skillet) or griddle pan and flatbreads were cooked over an open gas flame. Necessity was the name of the game but that didn't in anyway compromise the flavour of the food we ate at home.

Of course, over time things evolve and, having used an oven for over two decades, I now cannot see myself without one: it's such an essential part of our lifestyle. When I moved to the UK, my aim was always to bring the flavour of Indian food into my home kitchen. From the spices, tadkas, tikkas and breads to the chutneys, raita and salads. I have come to realize that the taste of 'home cooking' is less about where you live and more about the warmth and aromas of good food that fill the kitchen where you create these dishes. Striving day after day to recreate flavours and to understand more about spices, tastes, textures and consistency has always been my goal, satisfying my own curiosity and fuelling my knowledge. I am lucky enough to have the platform of my books, app and articles to be able to share all of it with you. As I continue to look back on my journey in food, there is no doubt that the dishes I enjoyed the most was the street food I ate when growing up in Mumbai. To be able to recreate a piece of that in my home kitchen fills me with joy. Sitting with family and friends around the dinner table, tucking into food that resonates with the flavours that remind me of 'home', well, I know that I'm on the right track.

In *Tandoori Home Cooking* I share recipes that I hope you will love cooking but also the tips and tricks that I have picked up over the years while eating my way across India, scouring the city streets for exciting dishes and cooking techniques: learning cooking skills that have been used for generations, but that have not always been widely known outside India. From spice blends and smoked butter to a double marination technique, which is the secret to a classic tikka, and cooking tandoori breads over a hob!

## THE SECRET TO A GOOD MARINADE

There is no set way to make a marinade. With ingredients as varied as meat, fish, vegetables and paneer, it's not a case of one size fits all. Zafrani Paneer Tikka (page 102) uses a marinade that is rich, creamy and includes ground spices, with saffron strands, fresh ginger, green chilli and fennel seeds all helping the paneer chunks to soak up flavour. The key to Adraki Tandoori Jhinge (page 77) is to include a mustard flavour in the short list of ingredients, which compliments the sweetness of the prawns as they cook. Marinades can be interchangeable, just keep in mind the type of protein or vegetable you are using and how that will help develop the flavours and how long they are given to soak up the goodness of the spices.

My Tandoori Chicken Tikka (page 24) uses a process known as the double marination technique (much like the Zafrani Paneer Tikka on page 102). The aim of this technique is to ensure you get as much flavour infused within the meat as possible via the first marinade and then the second marinade coats the outside of the chicken pieces. By doubling the quantity of the marinade it means that half the marinade can be used to coat the chicken before grilling while the other half of the marinade is then cooked separately and reduced down in consistency. Once the marinated chicken pieces have been grilled, they are then coated in this rich gravy to inject even more flavour and heat into the tikka morsels. It also ensures that once your tikkas are cooked they aren't dry when served. The double marination technique can be used for almost any recipe in this book; I have opted to use it for the more obvious ones where I feel it works best.

In Indian cooking, marination commonly follows a two-step process. The first marinade is usually garlic, ginger and an acidic element such as lemon juice or vinegar. Marinating chicken or lamb in this acidic mixture breaks down the meat tissues. Once the first marinade has done its work, it's followed by a second marinade that generally includes ground spices, green chilli and fresh herbs. The ingredients rest in the second marinade so the flavours are well absorbed: good-quality chicken, lamb and fish benefit from resting overnight as this tenderizes the meat further and make sure that, despite being cooked quickly over a high heat, the tikkas stay tender, moist, succulent and full of flavour. Tenderizers are commonly used. Although I have included a meat tenderizer in some recipes, it's not always essential. Natural tenderizers are also an option, including fresh ginger, pineapple and unripe papaya, all of which include enzymes that help break down the tissues in the meat so it absorbs the marinade and cooks well.

## SPICES AND SPICE BLENDS

Spices added to any marinade are key for the layers of flavour they lend to each dish. In some recipes I have used spice blends that are added right at the end. Sprinkling over a dry spice blend, such as chaat masala, before serving is one of the best ways to bring out the salty, tangy and warm notes of tikkas and kebabs. It's common practice at street stalls and one that I have included in my recipe for Aslam Butter Chicken (page 32) with the combination of chaat masala, black salt and chilli powder. It's a blend that you can use on any tikkas. As with my previous books, I believe the flavour you get from coarsely crushed spices compared to finely ground is miles apart and each again lends something unique to the recipe.

## DHUNGAR

The age-old technique known as dhungar is used to enhance a variety of dishes in Indian cooking to add that distinctive smoky flavour to kebabs, curries and even biryanis. To use the dhungar technique, create a small space in the centre of the bowl of uncooked tikka or kebab mixture. Add some ghee or melted butter to a small heatproof bowl and place it in the space you have created. Heat a piece of coal over an open flame to a high heat and then place the hot coal in the bowl with the ghee. As it begins to smoke, cover the larger bowl with a lid and leave the tikka or kebab mixture to take on the smoky flavour for at least 15 minutes. Once all the smoke has gone, continue to cook the dish as instructed. This does make the cooking time for any recipe slightly longer, but it's well worth the effort. If you are short on time, make a batch of my smoked butter (page 147) and use that for basting tikkas and kebabs to give a similar flavour achieved through the dhungar technique.

## CHUTNEYS

This book is brimming with chutneys! For Indians, chutney means a fresh, zingy condiment that is perfect for topping snacks and kebabs, served alongside salads. My favourite fresh chutneys and dips are definitely the Hari Mirch Ki Chutney (page 136), a fresh dip packed with heat from green chillies, lime and cumin, and the Sirkewalla Pyaz (page 143), a tangy chutney with onions, tamarind and chilli. Having lived in the UK for a long time, I now understand that the word chutney usually means a slow-cooked, generally fruit-based, jammy spread that is served with meats and cheese. In *Tandoori Home Cooking*, I have included a few slow-cooked, preserved chutneys. My absolute favourite is the Aam Chundo (page 131), a chutney that uses unripe mangoes along with chilli powder for a balance of tangy and hot tastes. You can opt for a fresh chutney or a preserved chutney as there are so many varieties to choose from. The preserved chutneys have a longer storage time, while the fresh ones also can be made in large batches and frozen.

## CREATING YOUR TANDOORI MEAL

There is a great variety of tandoori dishes on offer, including vegetarian recipes using ingredients like bell peppers and sweetcorn as well as yoghurt that can be strained and used to make kebabs (page 52). When it comes to accompaniments, tandoori dishes are served with flatbreads, chutneys, raitas and salads, all of which lend so much more to a meal when we eat a bite of a tikka or kebab. Dividing this book into chapters that truly reflect the main dishes and, perhaps more importantly, the sides was something I was keen to do and fills those pages with some true gems. The Santre ka Salaad (page 168), a spiced orange salad with green chilli and coriander, is so delicious and provides the perfect accompaniment to a rich tikka or kebab as it cuts through the tandoori flavours and lends an overall freshness. I have put together a few meal plans packed with vegan and vegetarian choices, alongside meat options, that you can find at the end of this book. I am someone who thrives on feeding those around me. Food is a comfort we all need and as we have seen through uncertain times is a constant in connecting us to one another. No matter the time of the year, the occasion or the number of guests around your dining table, I urge you to savour the flavours of *Tandoori Home Cooking*. I hope these recipes fill your meals with flavour, warmth and much joy for years to come.

INTRODUCTION

# Essential Ingredients

## ASAFOETIDA (HING)

Renowned for its digestive properties, asafoetida is a pungent spice from the ferula plant. Adding it to dishes lends a savoury note and it's always best used in smaller quantities. 'Hing', as it's also known, is sold in varying grades from mild to extra strong. Visiting one of Asia's large spice markets will give you an insight into the quality and aroma as well as the potency of this spice. Commonly a lot of stores in the UK sell asafoetida mixed with flour. Although this ensures a milder blend be aware it does affect the quality of the asafoetida.

## BLACK SALT (KALA NAMAK)

A pale grey-pink salt, also known as 'kala namak', is added to snacks, salad and kebabs to enhance the smokiness and aromas. Whole and ground varieties can vary in taste and colour. It's also great in drinks; I add it to my favourite spiced Indian lemonade, Banta Soda (page 195).

## CHAAT MASALA

A blend of spices including dried mango powder, black pepper, black salt, cumin and dried mint. Commonly sprinkled over tikkas, kebabs, salads, raita and even fresh fruit. Chaat masala is a taste sensation of sour, sweet, tangy and hot, all at once perking up dishes. It works particularly well when you prefer to avoid moisture in a dish. Adding the sour element to tikkas, snacks or fruit in place of lime juice. Or to amplify the flavour and use chaat masala alongside lime or lemon juice. You can make your own chaat masala though shop-bought varieties are equally good.

## CURRY LEAVES (KARIPATTA)

Also known as 'karipatta', curry leaves are available fresh in large bags from Asian grocers, although some large UK supermarkets are now stocking them too. If you do buy a large bag, curry leaves freeze really well — just make sure you use them straight from frozen to avoid discolouring. You can opt for dried curry leaves, but crush them first and then add them to dishes at the end of cooking.

## DRIED FENUGREEK LEAVES (KASOORI METHI)

Widely used in Indian cooking, dried fenugreek leaves or 'kasoori methi' have a wonderful savoury and slightly bitter flavour. Added to kebabs, curries and marinades, they lend a wonderful warmth and mellow taste. Coarsely grind the dried leaves in a pestle and mortar to extract the most flavour.

## DRIED MANGO POWDER (AMCHOOR)

Also known as 'amchoor', dried mango powder is made from raw mangoes and is beige in colour with a wonderful citrusy tang to it. It's great to add to tikkas just as they are served warm or even to salads. Dried mango powder lends a fruity, sour note and is readily available in Indian grocers or online.

## DRIED POMEGRANATE POWDER (ANARDANA)

The powder is made by pounding dried pomegranate seeds, or 'anardana', and lends a refreshing, sour fruitiness to dishes. It's coarse in texture and works really well when added to salads and kebabs. Pomegranates have been used in Indian cooking for years in a variety of forms, including fresh seeds, juice and molasses.

## GARAM MASALA

A blend of spices added during or after the dish is made. Whole spices are toasted in a dry pan to release their essential oils, enhancing all the flavour and warmth. The garam masala blend varies within each region (and even community). Below is my family recipe, which has been part of our home cooking for over 60 years. This is my go-to blend for most recipes that require garam masala, however, where a particular blend is listed in the ingredients, such as for the Aslam Butter Chicken (page 32), then use that specified blend for the best results.

MAKES 50 G (2 OZ)

8 cm (3 in) cassia bark or cinnamon stick
3 heaped tbsp coriander seeds
2 tbsp green cardamom pods (seeds only)
½ tbsp cloves
1 tbsp black peppercorn
4 black cardamom pods (seeds only)

Add all the spices to a dry frying pan (skillet) over a low heat. Toast for 6–7 minutes, frequently shaking the pan. Allow the spices to cool and then grind to a fine powder in a spice grinder. Store in an airtight container until ready to use.

## GREEN CARDAMOM (ELAICHI / VELCHI)

Also known as 'elaichi' in Hindi or 'velchi' in Marathi; green cardamom is one of the most versatile spices in Indian cooking. It's a spice that is picked just before ripening so the pods don't split. From savoury to sweet dishes and even in drinks, it's used whole, coarsely crushed and ground to a fine powder. All forms bring a varied flavour profile; the ground variety has a stronger flavour so you need to use it sparingly.

## KASHMIRI CHILLI POWDER

Anyone who has followed my recipes will know I am biased towards using Kashmiri chilli powder, a bright red variety of chilli with both smoky and citrusy notes. Compared to the variety of chillies across India — Guntur, Byadgi or Resham Patti, to name a few — these are mildly spicy with a vibrant colour. The colour renders itself through marinades, chilli oils and dressings, so you can get away with adding a touch more. If you are unable to get hold of Kashmiri chilli powder, I suggest opting for a mild (unsmoked) paprika to provide the vibrant colour and then adding a pinch of cayenne pepper to supply the required heat for the dish.

## MEAT TENDERIZER POWDER

Known commonly as 'Kachri powder', it contains papain from the papaya fruit. Meat tenderizer helps to break down the tough fibres in meat.

## MUSTARD OIL

I use mustard oil in recipes to bring a distinct pungent flavour; it's perfect in chutneys, tikkas and stir fries. Mustard oil is also used for its preservative properties when making pickles to increase the shelf life.

## PANEER

A classic Indian cheese that is the perfect vehicle to soak up the flavours and aromas from spices in curries and kebabs. Paneer cooks quickly, has a crumbly texture but when cooked holds its shape. It has been part of the vegetarian diet across Indian communities for generations. You can make paneer just with milk and lemon juice although lots of supermarkets nowadays stock good-quality paneer.

## SHREDDED COCONUT

Shredded or grated coconut is available to buy frozen, stocked in the freezer aisle of Asian grocers and larger supermarkets. I usually keep a few packs in my freezer and use this frozen coconut for fresh chutneys and stir fries. When cooking, it's far easier to dip into a pack, rather than break open a fresh coconut! You can always opt for desiccated coconut if you cannot get hold of either frozen or fresh. To reintroduce moisture before using, soak the desiccated coconut in hot water for 15–20 minutes. Drain the water and use the coconut as directed in the recipe.

## TAMARIND PASTE

Tamarind is extracted from pods and can be bought as a paste, concentrate or in blocks. It acts as a souring agent in cooking. As I mention in my recipes, make sure you check the quality and strength of your tamarind paste to ensure that you have the right amount of tang required. If it's too strong, add a little less. If it's too weak, add a tad more.

# CHICKEN

There are many types of chicken tikka, a term that is celebrated in its essence through the sheer variety of recipes in this chapter. Each dish is packed with complex flavours and aromas from the marinades, spice mixes and butter basting. When it comes to chicken skewers, I opt to use chicken thighs. Not only is it a tender cut that doesn't tend to dry out during cooking, it's also more cost effective than other cuts. From the simplest recipes that are ideal for a midweek dinner to the absolutely showstopping Murgh Musallam (page 43) for your festive table, I'm hoping this chapter gives a glimpse into how tandoori food has historically included influences of diverse regions, from the use of spices to unique cooking techniques.

# Creamy Chicken Skewers with Green Chilli & Coriander

## MURGH MALAI TIKKA

These creamy chicken skewers are marinated in yoghurt and cream with garlic, ginger, green chillies and coriander (cilantro). Adding a rich coating to the chicken, the secret to this marinade is grated (shredded) cheese, which clings to the meat as it cooks under a hot grill. This versatile marinade is a malai tandoori recipe — the word 'malai' means cream — and can be used for vegetarian dishes too. I love cooking cauliflower florets in the same marinade. I serve these chicken tikkas with a sprinkling of chaat masala, although you can add a squeeze of lime juice instead.

You will need wooden skewers soaked in cold water for 30 minutes

640 g (1 lb 6½ oz) boneless, skinless chicken thighs, cut into bite-size pieces
melted butter, for basting
pinch of garam masala
pinch of chaat masala

### For the marinade

5 garlic cloves, roughly chopped
5 cm (2 in) ginger root, roughly chopped
2 green bird's-eye chillies
2 tbsp malt vinegar
2 tbsp Greek yoghurt
80 ml (2¾ fl oz) double (heavy) cream
1 tsp cornflour (cornstarch)
30 g (1 oz) cheddar cheese, grated (shredded)
handful of coriander (cilantro) leaves, finely chopped

To make the marinade, grind the garlic, ginger and chillies in a blender with a splash of water to a smooth paste. Put this paste in a large mixing bowl with the vinegar, then add the chicken. Leave to marinate for 30 minutes.

In a separate small bowl, combine the yoghurt, cream and cornflour (cornstarch). Mix well to get rid of any lumps. Add the cheese and coriander (cilantro). Season to taste and stir well. Add this yoghurt mixture to the bowl with the marinated chicken pieces. Mix well and leave to marinate in the fridge for at least 1 hour or preferably overnight.

Preheat the grill (broiler) to a medium heat. Line a baking tray with foil and place a wire rack over the tray.

Thread the chicken pieces onto the soaked wooden skewers and place them on the wire rack. Top the skewers with any leftover marinade. Place the tray under the grill and cook for 7–8 minutes. Baste with the melted butter, then turn the skewers and grill for a further 8 minutes until the chicken is lightly charred around the edges and cooked through.

Take the chicken off the skewers and serve on a large platter, topped with garam masala and chaat masala. Serve with pickled chillies, red onions and naan.

# Tandoori Chicken Tikka

Some classics are hard to resist. This tandoori chicken tikka has been a constant in my cooking repertoire for as long as I can remember. I use the double marination technique here. Of course, you can grill the skewers without doubling up on the marinade to coat the chicken at the end — it will turn out just as tasty. You can amp up the flavour even further by using my smoked butter (page 147) to baste the chicken. When you crave a good old tandoori chicken tikka, this is the recipe to turn to.

You will need wooden skewers soaked in cold water for 30 minutes

640 g (1 lb 6½ oz) boneless, skinless chicken thighs, cut into bite-size pieces
butter, for basting and cooking
juice of ½ lime
generous pinch of chaat masala

### For the marinade
3 garlic cloves
2.5 cm (1 in) ginger root, peeled
6 tbsp Greek yoghurt
2 heaped tsp chickpea (gram) flour
1½ tsp Kashmiri chilli powder
¼ tsp garam masala
2 tsp ground coriander
½ tsp ground cinnamon
½ tsp saffron strands, crushed
1 tbsp dried fenugreek leaves (*kasoori methi*), crushed
pinch of sugar
salt, to taste

To make the marinade, grind the garlic and ginger with a splash of water in a blender to a smooth paste. In a large mixing bowl, combine the yoghurt with the chickpea (gram) flour. Mix well to get rid of any lumps and form a thick paste. Add the ginger and garlic paste, chilli powder, garam masala, coriander, cinnamon, saffron, dried fenugreek, sugar and salt. Stir well, mixing everything to a smooth consistency.

Put 2 tablespoons of the marinade in a small bowl and set aside.

Add the chicken to the bowl and mix well to make sure each piece is coated in the thick marinade. Cover the bowl and leave to marinate in the fridge for 2–3 hours, or preferably overnight.

Preheat the grill (broiler) to a medium heat. Line a baking tray with foil and place a wire rack over the tray.

Thread the chicken pieces onto the soaked wooden skewers and place them on the wire rack. Place the tray under the grill and cook for 17–18 minutes. Turn the skewers halfway through the cooking time and baste with the melted butter until the chicken is lightly charred around the edges and cooked through.

Meanwhile, transfer the reserved marinade to a small frying pan (skillet). Place over a medium heat and cook, stirring continuously, for 5 minutes until the marinade reduces and thickens. Add 2 teaspoons butter and turn off the heat. Transfer the cooked marinade to a bowl.

Take the chicken off the skewers and add it to the bowl with the marinade along with the lime juice and chaat masala. Stir well to make sure the chicken is evenly coated. Serve warm with salad and naan or roti.

# Sesame–Coated Chicken Skewers with Green Chilli & Black Pepper

**TILL KA TIKKA**

Bite-size pieces of chicken are marinated in peppery yoghurt, then coated in batter and rolled in sesame seeds before being skewered and grilled over a high heat until lightly charred. The sesame seed crust turns crispy and nutty with a hint of heat from the green chillies in the batter.

You will need wooden skewers soaked in cold water for 30 minutes

600 g (1 lb 5 oz) boneless, skinless chicken thighs, cut into bite-size pieces
white sesame seeds, for coating
melted butter, for basting

### For the marinade

4 garlic cloves
2 green bird's-eye chillies
3 tbsp Greek yoghurt
1 tsp ground cardamom
1 tsp ground black pepper
pinch of salt

### For the batter

6 green bird's-eye chillies
60 g (2 oz/½ cup) plain (all-purpose) flour
2 eggs
4 tbsp chopped coriander (cilantro) leaves
salt, to taste

To make the marinade, pound the garlic and chillies to a paste in a pestle and mortar, or use a grater. Put this paste in a large mixing bowl and add the yoghurt, cardamom, pepper and salt. Add the chicken to the bowl and mix well to make sure each piece is coated in the marinade. Cover the bowl and leave to marinate in the fridge for 2–3 hours, or preferably overnight.

To make the batter, crush the green chillies and put them in a large mixing bowl. Add all the remaining ingredients and whisk to a thick batter.

Preheat the grill (broiler) to a medium heat. Line a baking tray with foil and place a wire rack over the tray. Brush the wire rack with oil.

Place the sesame seeds in a small bowl. Take the chicken pieces out of the marinade, dip them first in the batter and then coat them in the sesame seeds. Thread the chicken pieces onto the soaked wooden skewers and place them on the wire rack. This might be messy, but it's worth it! Place the tray under the hot grill on the top shelf and cook for 6–7 minutes. Baste with melted butter and continue cooking for further 5 minutes until the sesame seeds go nutty and brown.

Take the chicken off the skewers and serve on a large platter with tawa roti and a fresh chutney.

# Chicken Skewers Marinated in Fenugreek, Turmeric & Garlic

## MURGH METHI TIKKA

Using both fresh and dried fenugreek in this chicken tikka recipe lends a freshness and a savoury note to the marinade. Using Greek yoghurt in the marinade ensures a rich, creamy consistency that coats the chicken well. The chicken skewers are finished with chaat masala, which is a classic tangy spice mix added at the end once it is cooked.

You will need wooden skewers soaked in cold water for 30 minutes

500 g (1 lb 2 oz) boneless, skinless chicken thighs, cut into bite-size pieces
5 garlic cloves
5 cm (2 in) ginger root
2 tbsp malt vinegar
melted butter, for basting
pinch of chilli powder
pinch of chaat masala

### For the marinade

240 g (8½ oz) Greek yoghurt
2 tsp chickpea (gram) flour
2 tbsp finely chopped fresh methi leaves
1 tbsp dried fenugreek leaves (*kasoori methi*)
1 tbsp ground coriander
½ tsp ground turmeric
1 tbsp mustard oil
salt, to taste

Blitz the garlic, ginger and vinegar to a paste in a blender. Put this paste in a large mixing bowl and add the chicken. Mix well and set aside.

In a separate mixing bowl, combine all the marinade ingredients and stir well. Pour half of this marinade over the chicken in the large bowl and mix well to make sure each piece is fully coated. Cover both bowls and leave them to marinate in the fridge for at least 6 hours, or preferably overnight.

Preheat the grill (broiler) to a medium-high heat. Line a baking tray with foil and place a wire rack over the tray.

Put the reserved marinade in a non-stick saucepan with 50 ml (1¾ fl oz) of water. Cook over a medium heat for 5 minutes, stirring continuously until it thickens and cooks through. Transfer this cooked marinade to a mixing bowl and set aside.

Thread the chicken pieces onto the soaked wooden skewers and place them on the wire rack. Place the tray under the grill and cook for 6 minutes. Baste with melted butter and grill for a further 6–7 minutes until the chicken is lightly charred around the edges and cooked through.

Take the chicken off the skewers and add it to the bowl of reserved marinade, sprinkle with chilli powder and chaat masala, then stir well. Arrange the chicken on a serving platter and serve warm with flatbread and some chutney.

# Spiced Chicken Skewers with Pickling Spices, Mustard & Chilli

## ACHARI MURGH TIKKA

I'm such a fan of achari spice mix that all my books include recipes that celebrate it. Achari Murgh Tikka has always been a family favourite. I first ate it as a young girl when our family visited Khyber at Fort in Mumbai, where it always feels like a special evening and the food is delicious. The decor is old school with painted murals on the walls that are dimly lit by decorative chandeliers from the '80s. Ghazals play in the background with chatter from the tables. It's like going back in time to your safe space. The menu is limited and focuses primarily on the cuisine from the north-west frontier of India. The achari spice mix includes fennel, cumin, mustard and nigella seeds, all coarsely crushed, but the secret is definitely using mustard oil. I recommend keeping a small bottle in your storecupboard. The pungent, savoury flavour lends an intense taste to the tikka.

You will need wooden skewers soaked in cold water for 30 minutes

640 g (1 lb 6½ oz) boneless, skinless chicken thighs, cut into bite-size pieces
2 tbsp butter
2 tbsp chickpea (gram) flour
1 tbsp mustard oil
3 tbsp Greek yoghurt
salt, to taste
melted butter, to baste
juice of ½ lime, to garnish

### For the marinade

6 garlic cloves
5 cm (2 in) ginger root
1 heaped tsp Kashmiri chilli powder (or mild chilli powder)
juice of ½ lime

### For the spice mix

1½ tsp fennel seeds
1½ tsp cumin seeds
1½ tsp black mustard seeds
1 tsp nigella seeds
½ tsp fenugreek seeds

To make the marinade, grind the garlic and ginger with a splash of water in a blender to a smooth paste. Put this paste in a large mixing bowl with the chilli powder and lime juice, then add the chicken. Mix well and leave to marinate for 20 minutes.

Heat a small, dry frying pan (skillet) over a medium heat. Put all the spice mix ingredients in the pan and toast for 2 minutes, shaking the pan a few times. Transfer the toasted spices to a small bowl and set aside to cool.

Using the same pan, melt the butter over a medium heat and then add the chickpea (gram) flour. Stirring well to get rid of any lumps, roast the flour for about 2–3 minutes, or until it has a nutty aroma and changes colour.

Once cool, grind the toasted spices to a coarse powder in a pestle and mortar. Add the toasted spice mix to the marinated chicken along with the roasted chickpea flour mixture, mustard oil and yoghurt. Season to taste. Leave to marinate in the fridge for 2 hours, or preferably overnight.

Preheat the grill (broiler) to a medium-high heat. Line a baking tray with foil and place a wire rack over the tray.

Thread the chicken pieces onto the soaked wooden skewers and place them on the wire rack. Place the tray under the grill and cook for 16–18 minutes, turning halfway through cooking and basting with the melted butter, until the chicken is lightly charred around the edges and cooked through.

Take the chicken off the skewers and serve on a large platter with the lime juice squeezed over. Serve with roti, pickled chillies and green chutney.

# Spiced Green Chicken Skewers with Mint, Coriander & Chilli

## HARYALI MURGH TIKKA

Marinating meats and vegetables in fresh green herbs is common practice in tandoori cooking. The vibrant colour of these chicken skewers — the word 'haryali' means green — comes from the addition of the green herbs, chillies and bell pepper to the paste. I have opted for the classic combination of mint, coriander (cilantro) and bird's-eye chillies, but I have also included my secret ingredient of green bell pepper to add more depth to the marinade and strengthen the colour.

You will need wooden skewers soaked in cold water for 30 minutes

750 g (1 lb 10½ oz) boneless, skinless chicken thighs, cut into bite-size pieces
melted butter, for basting
chaat masala, to garnish

### For the marinade

4 garlic cloves
2.5 cm (1 in) ginger root, roughly chopped
juice of ½ lime
pinch of salt
3 tbsp Greek yoghurt
¼ tsp ground turmeric
½ tsp garam masala
¼ tsp coarsely ground black pepper
salt, to taste

### For the paste

50 g (1¾ oz) mint leaves
50 g (1¾ oz) coriander (cilantro) leaves and stems
2 green bird's-eye chillies
120 g (4¼ oz) green bell pepper

To make the marinade, grind the garlic and ginger in a blender with a splash of water to a smooth paste. Put this paste in a large mixing bowl with the lime juice and a pinch of salt, then add the chicken. Mix well and leave to marinate for 20 minutes.

Put all the paste ingredients in a blender along with 1 tablespoon of the yoghurt and blend to a smooth paste. Add this paste to the bowl with the marinated chicken pieces along with the remaining yoghurt, turmeric, garam masala, black pepper and salt. Mix well and leave to marinate in the fridge for 1 hour, or preferably overnight.

Preheat the grill (broiler) to a medium-high heat. Line a baking tray with foil and place a wire rack over the tray.

Thread the chicken pieces onto the soaked wooden skewers and place them on the wire rack. Cook the skewers in batches, if necessary. Place the tray under the grill and cook for 8–9 minutes. Baste with the melted butter, turn the skewers and grill for a further 8–9 minutes, basting with the melted butter again, until the chicken is lightly charred around the edges and cooked through.

Take the chicken off the skewers and serve on a large platter with the chaat masala sprinkled over. Serve with naan or roti, salad and chutney.

# Spiced Butter Chicken with Garlic, Chilli & Chaat Masala

## ASLAM BUTTER CHICKEN

I have cooked butter chicken for years and there are over 4 million of you who love my recipe after watching it online. Even though that recipe is an absolute hit, I want to share this alternative butter chicken as it's a true gem. Amidst the busy narrow streets of Old Delhi is a little shop in the heart of Jama Masjid called Aslam Chicken. The low-key restaurant gives no clues to the robust taste that you are about to delve into. It's only fitting to celebrate this iconic space with a recipe that I know you will love. This isn't like a regular butter chicken, although the dish is smothered in an obscene amount of butter!

700 g (1 lb 8½ oz) boneless, skinless chicken thighs, cut into bite-size pieces
melted butter, for basting

### For the marinade

3 tbsp Greek yoghurt
5 garlic cloves, roughly chopped
2.5 cm (1 in) ginger root, roughly chopped
1 tsp dried fenugreek leaves (*kasoori methi*)
2 tbsp malt vinegar
salt, to taste

### For the garam masala

1 tbsp coriander seeds
1 tsp cumin seeds
4 cloves
4 green cardamom pods (seeds only)
2 mace blades
2.5 cm (1 in) cinnamon stick
2 dried mild red chillies

### For smoking the chicken (optional)

1 piece of coal
3 cloves
1 tsp ghee

### To assemble

1 tsp chaat masala
¼ tsp black salt
¼ tsp Kashmiri chilli powder
70 ml (2¼ fl oz) soured cream
2 tbsp single (light) cream
50 g (2 oz) melted butter

To make the garam masala, heat a dry frying pan (skillet) over a medium heat. Add all the spices and dried chillies to the hot pan and toast for 3–4 minutes. Set aside to cool.

Once cool, grind the toasted spices in a blender to a fine powder. To make the marinade, add 1 tablespoon of the yoghurt, the garlic, ginger and dried fenugreek leaves to the blender with the garam masala. Blitz to a fine paste.

Put the chicken in a large mixing bowl and add the marinade along with the remaining yoghurt and the vinegar. Season to taste. Mix well to make sure each piece of chicken is coated in the marinade.

Next, smoke the chicken. Create a small well in the middle of the chicken large enough to place a small bowl. Using tongs, heat the coal over a very hot flame. Once hot, carefully put the coal in a small heatproof, non-reactive bowl. While hot, add the cloves and ghee to the bowl. The coal will begin to smoke as you add the ghee. Nestle the small bowl in the well made inside the bowl of chicken. Cover the large bowl and leave for 1 hour to let the smoke infuse the chicken. Remove the small bowl of coal, re-cover the large bowl and leave the chicken to marinate in the fridge overnight.

Put the chaat masala, black salt and chilli powder in a small bowl and set aside. In a separate bowl mix together the soured cream and single (light) cream and set aside.

Preheat the grill (broiler) to a medium heat. Line a baking tray with foil and place a wire rack over the tray.

Thread the chicken pieces onto the soaked wooden skewers and place them on the wire rack. Place the tray under the grill and cook for 8 minutes. Baste with butter, turn the skewers and grill for a further 8–9 minutes until the chicken is lightly charred around the edges and cooked through.

Take the chicken off the skewers and serve in a large bowl, topped with chaat masala blend and a splash of cream. Pour over as much or as little melted butter as you like, then stir well. Serve with roti.

Aslam Butter Chicken

CHICKEN

# Tandoori Chicken Wings
# with Tamarind & Chilli

Sticky chicken wings are such a crowd pleaser. These are coated in the ultimate tamarind-chilli sauce that lends a sweet, sour, tangy and spicy flavour to the wings. Tamarind paste gives a rich deep colour to the chicken while adding a wonderful tartness. Make sure to check the strength of the paste and adjust the amount used as required. In my marinade, I normally use jaggery (Indian cane sugar), although here I have swapped it for soft dark brown sugar as that is more readily available.

4 tbsp cornflour (cornstarch)
2 tbsp rice flour
½ tsp garlic powder
pinch of salt
12 chicken wings
green bird's-eye chillies,
    slit lengthwise, to serve

### For the tamarind sauce

5 tbsp soft dark brown sugar
1 tsp Kashmiri chilli powder
6 tbsp tamarind paste (check the
    strength and adjust to taste)
2 tbsp vegetable oil

Preheat the oven to 200°C fan (425°F/gas 7). Line a baking tray with parchment paper.

Mix together the cornflour (cornstarch), rice flour, garlic powder and salt in a bowl and set aside.

To make the tamarind sauce, put the sugar, chilli powder and 200 ml (6¾ fl oz/¾ cup) of water in a small saucepan and simmer over a low heat for 2–3 minutes. Add the tamarind paste and oil and continue to simmer, stirring continuously, for a further 3 minutes as the sauce thickens. Turn off the heat and set aside to cool.

Dip the chicken wings in the flour mixture so they are evenly coated and then place on the baking tray. Place the tray in the hot oven and bake the chicken for 40 minutes, turning the wings over halfway through the cooking time. Remove the wings from the oven, put them in a bowl and pour over the tamarind sauce while still warm.

Arrange the chicken wings on a serving platter and serve with any extra sauce and green chillies, alongside roti and salad.

# Saffron–Spiced Whole Roast Chicken

## ZAFRANI MURGH

Saffron has long exerted its influence across regions of India: it's a staple ingredient not just in curries and biryanis but also in tandoori cooking. The spiced yoghurt and almond marinade coats the chicken, infusing the meat. The chicken is then basted with the saffron-flavoured ghee or butter as it cooks all the way through to keep the whole bird moist, lend even more flavour and give everything a wonderful golden colour.

1 tsp saffron strands
200 g (7 oz) ghee or butter
1.9 kg (4 lb 3 oz) whole chicken

### For the marinade

220 g (7¾ oz) Greek yoghurt
3 tsp ground almonds
   (almond meal)
2 tsp Kashmiri chilli powder
2 tsp ground cardamom
½ tsp ground cinnamon
8 garlic cloves, ground to a paste
5 cm (2 in) ginger root, ground
   to a paste
salt, to taste

In a mixing bowl, crush the saffron strands, add the ghee or butter and mix well. Divide this saffron ghee between two bowls. Set one bowl aside to use for basting the chicken during roasting.

Place the chicken on a large plate and, starting at the neck end, ease the skin away from the flesh. Spread the saffron ghee from the second bowl under and over the skin.

In a separate bowl, combine the yoghurt, almonds, chilli powder, cardamom, cinnamon, garlic and ginger pastes. Season to taste. Spread this marinade over the chicken and leave to marinate in the fridge for at least 2 hours, or preferably overnight.

Preheat the oven to 180°C fan (400°F/gas 6). Line a roasting tray with foil and place a wire rack over the tray.

Sit the chicken breast side up on the wire rack. The tray will collect all the juices from the chicken as it cooks. Place the tray in the hot oven and roast the chicken for 45 minutes. Baste the chicken with the reserved saffron ghee, then turn the chicken over so it is breast side down and continue to roast for a further 50 minutes. Once the chicken is cooked through and the juices are running clear, turn off the oven. Transfer the chicken to a large serving plate. As you lift the chicken, let any juices from the cavity pour into the roasting tray — you can use these juices to make a light gravy. Cover the chicken loosely with foil and leave to rest in a warm place for 20–30 minutes.

Carve the chicken and arrange the pieces on a serving platter. Serve warm with spiced vegetables or salads.

# Whole Roast Chicken Cooked in Yoghurt with Mustard & Garam Masala

**DAK BUNGALOW ROAST CHICKEN**

As the name signifies, this recipe is influenced by the Dak Bungalow chicken curry from the east of India, which was created for visitors who frequented the local guest houses (bungalows) during the British Raj. A regional Bengali variation uses mustard oil for a delicious pungency, although I have swapped it for English mustard in this recipe to give that required savoury flavour.

1 kg (2 lb 3 oz) whole chicken
3 tbsp ghee or butter, for
　basting

### For the marinade

2 tbsp Greek yoghurt
1½ tsp Kashmiri chilli powder
½ tsp ground turmeric
1 tbsp ground coriander
½ tsp garam masala
1 tsp sugar
3 tsp English mustard
1 heaped tbsp garlic and ginger
　paste (4 garlic cloves and
　5 cm/2 in ginger root)
1 tbsp vegetable oil
salt, to taste

Combine all the marinade ingredients in a mixing bowl. Place the chicken on a large plate and using your hands spread the marinade onto the chicken until the skin is fully covered. Leave to marinate in the fridge for at least 4 hours, or preferably overnight. If you want to, you can cover the chicken with a dome made out of foil.

Take the chicken out of the fridge and leave at room temperature for an hour before cooking.

Preheat the oven to 180°C fan (400°F/gas 6). Line a deep baking tray with foil and place a wire rack over the tray.

Sit the chicken on the wire rack. The tray will collect all the juices from the chicken as it cooks. Place the tray in the hot oven and roast the chicken for 1 hour 10 minutes. Baste the chicken with the ghee every 20 minutes to make sure the meat is moist. Once the chicken is cooked through and the juices are running clear, turn off the oven. Take the Dak Bungalow chicken out of the oven, cover loosely with foil and leave to rest in a warm place for 15 minutes.

Carve the chicken and arrange the pieces on a serving platter. Serve with potatoes, sides and chutney.

# Whole Roast Chicken Stuffed with Mince, Cashews, Raisins, Green Chillies & Boiled Eggs

## MURGH MUSALLAM

The literal translation of 'murgh musallam' is whole chicken. A classic dish from the city of Lucknow influenced by the Mughals, whose impact spread from the east of India, across Awadh and through to Lucknow. Indulgent recipes were such an integral part of Mughal culture and this recipe is a reflection of their grand banquets where ostentatious platters of food were served to royals. These recipes in particular have left a lasting impression: the cooking techniques and use of spices, how each singular spice has its place even in the lengthiest recipes. Stuffing the bird with minced (ground) chicken, which has been cooked in ghee with nuts and spices, helps to keep the juices in the whole chicken and lends so much more flavour to the meat. Although in the traditional recipe the eggs are stuffed inside the whole chicken, I prefer to use them as a garnish so it's easier to carve when you are ready to serve. Give yourself plenty of time to make this dish and equally to indulge in the eating of it. If necessary, the stuffing and the gravy can be made a day ahead. I was hesitant in sharing something quite so grand, but this is such a part of Indian heritage that passing it down feels like a fitting way of celebrating our culinary history.

Recipe overleaf  ⟶

## For the chicken

3 tbsp ghee or vegetable oil
400 g (14 oz) white onions,
    thinly sliced
1.7 kg (3 lb 12 oz) whole chicken
pinch of saffron strands
1 tsp rose water
ghee, for basting
3 boiled eggs, to serve

## For the marinade

1 tsp white poppy seeds
6 green cardamom pods
    (seeds only)
5 cloves
2 tbsp cashew nuts
4 tbsp Greek yoghurt
5 garlic cloves
5 cm (2 in) ginger root
1 tsp Kashmiri chilli powder
1 tsp garam masala
1 tbsp ground coriander
20 g (¾ oz) mint leaves,
    finely chopped
2 tbsp lemon juice
salt, to taste
1 tsp meat tenderizer (optional)

## For the stuffing

2 green bird's-eye chillies,
    finely chopped
½ tsp ground coriander
½ tsp ground turmeric
150 g (5¼ oz) minced (ground)
    chicken
salt, to taste
1 tbsp finely chopped coriander
    (cilantro) leaves
1 tbsp cashew nuts,
    roughly crushed
1 tbsp raisins

## For the gravy

1 tsp ghee
100 ml (3½ fl oz/scant ½ cup)
    water

Heat the ghee or oil in a large frying pan (skillet) over a medium heat. Add the onions and fry for 30–35 minutes, stirring occasionally, until soft and brown. Transfer half the caramelized onions to a plate and leave to cool.

Continue cooking the remaining onions in the pan to prepare the stuffing. Add the green chillies to the pan with the onions and fry for just a few seconds. Add the ground coriander and turmeric, stir well, then add the minced (ground) chicken, stir again, lower the heat and cook for 1 minute. Season to taste. Add the coriander (cilantro) leaves, cashew nuts and raisins. Turn off the heat, stir well and set aside while you make the marinade.

To make the marinade, add the poppy seeds, cardamom, cloves and cashew nuts to a small, dry frying pan and toast for 1–2 minutes. Put the toasted spices in a blender and add the reserved caramelized onions, 3 tablespoons of the yoghurt, the garlic, ginger, chilli powder, garam masala and ground coriander. Blend to a smooth, thick paste. Scrape this into a large mixing bowl and add the mint, lemon juice, salt and meat tenderizer, if using. Divide the marinade between two bowls.

Place the whole chicken on a large plate. Fill the cavity of the chicken with the stuffing and tie the legs. Next, spread half the marinade all over the chicken and under the skin. Leave to marinate in the fridge overnight.

Mix together the saffron and rose water in a small bowl and set aside.

Preheat the oven to 180°C fan (400°F/gas 6). Line a roasting tray with foil and place a wire rack over the tray.

Sit the chicken breast side up on the wire rack. The tray will collect all the juices from the chicken as it cooks. Place the tray in the hot oven and roast the chicken for 45 minutes. Baste the chicken with ghee halfway through the cooking time, then turn the chicken over so it is breast side down, baste again and continue to roast for a further 50 minutes.

Once the chicken is cooked through and the juices are running clear, turn off the oven. Transfer the chicken to a large plate. As you lift the chicken, let any juices from the cavity pour into the roasting tray — use these to make a light gravy. Drizzle the saffron rose water over the chicken. Cover the chicken loosely with foil and leave to rest for 20–30 minutes while you make the gravy.

To make the gravy, heat the ghee in a small saucepan over a low heat. Add the leftover marinade, chicken juices from the roasting tin and water. Stir and simmer for 15–20 minutes until the gravy thickens.

Carve the chicken and arrange the pieces on a large serving platter. Serve with the warm gravy and halved boiled eggs, alongside chargrilled green beans or a salad, such as my Apple, Beetroot and Mooli Salad.

# LAMB

Over years of cooking Indian recipes, I have realized that, alongside spices, it's good-quality meat that really makes the recipe a winner. My recipe for Kandahari Gosht Tikka (page 60) is all about getting maximum flavour from a minimal list of ingredients. I have opted for using meat tenderizers in some recipes, but again, it's optional and not really needed as long as the lamb is given enough time to marinate in the spices.

# Spicy Lamb Chops Marinated in Garlic, Chilli & Garam Masala

## CHAAMP MASALA

Whenever she wanted to serve up something truly special for dinner parties at our family home in Mumbai, my mum would always make these masala lamb chops. Adding Worcestershire sauce (a must-have ingredient in a lot of Parsi dishes) to the marinade gives a lovely umami flavour to the lamb along with the garlic, ginger and ground spices. I opt to use a shop-bought chilli-garlic sauce that has a vibrant red colour and the perfect consistency to coat the meat. Adjust the quantity of the chilli-garlic sauce depending on how spicy it is. Cooked in the oven, the rich marinade clings to the lightly charred chops.

8 lamb chops (French trimmed)
smoked butter (page 147),
    for basting

### For the marinade

3 garlic cloves
5 cm (2 in) ginger root
2 green bird's-eye chillies
2 tbsp shop-bought chilli-garlic
    sauce (I use the Lee Kum
    Kee brand)
2 tbsp Worcestershire sauce
1½ tsp ground coriander
1 tsp Kashmiri chilli powder
¼ tsp garam masala
salt, to taste

Put the garlic, ginger and chillies in a blender with a splash of water and blend to a smooth paste. Put this paste in a deep dish along with the chilli garlic sauce, Worcestershire sauce, ground coriander, chilli powder and garam masala. Season with just a little salt. Add the lamb chops to the dish and mix well to make sure each chop is coated in the marinade. Leave to marinate in the fridge overnight.

Preheat the oven to 200°C fan (425°F/gas 7). Line a baking tray with foil and place a wire rack over the tray.

Place the chops on the wire rack. Place the tray in the hot oven and cook for 35–40 minutes. Halfway through the cooking time, baste the chops with the smoked butter and return to the oven to continue cooking.

Serve the lamb chops warm with roti and mint raita.

# Tandoori Lamb Chops with Yoghurt, Chilli & Nutmeg

## LAMB BURRA KEBAB

Lamb burra kebabs — which translates as 'best end chops' — are synonymous with every tandoori street stall across India, including in Old Delhi at Karim's. Mutton chops are traditionally used, although I have swapped it for lamb in this recipe, that are cooked on skewers in a tandoor so there is an even dry heat across the chops. Here I have cooked the chops on a high grill setting, which gives a wonderful charred flavour. Setting the chops on a wire rack ensures the heat circulates around the base of the chop too. The ground spice mix including mace and black cardamom is my favourite and complements this burra kebab recipe perfectly.

5 garlic cloves
5 cm (2 in) ginger root
1 heaped tsp Kashmiri chilli
    powder
2 tbsp malt vinegar
8 lamb chops
smoked butter (page 147),
    for basting
mint raita (page 141), to serve

### For the garam masala

1 tsp cumin seeds
6 cloves
½ tsp whole black peppercorns
2 black cardamom pods
    (seeds only)
2 mace blades

### For the yoghurt marinade

3 tbsp Greek yoghurt
1 tsp ground nutmeg
2 tbsp mustard oil
salt, to taste

The day before, blitz all the garam masala ingredients in a blender to a coarse powder and set aside.

Blend the garlic and ginger in the same blender with a splash of water to a smooth paste. Put this paste in a large mixing bowl with the chilli powder and malt vinegar, then add the lamb chops and massage in the marinade. Mix well and leave to marinate for 1 hour.

In a small bowl, combine the yoghurt marinade ingredients with the garam masala blend, mix well and spread this second marinade across each lamb chop. Now cover the bowl and marinate in the fridge overnight so the chops soak up all the flavours.

Preheat the grill (broiler) to a high heat. Line a baking tray with foil and place a wire rack over the tray.

Place the lamb chops on the wire rack. Place the tray under the hot grill and cook for 5 minutes, basting with the smoked butter. Flip the chops over and continue to grill for a further 7–8 minutes until lightly charred around the edges.

Serve with mint raita and salad.

# Spiced Lamb Cutlets with Spinach, Ginger, Chilli & Chaat Masala

ADRAKI CHAAMP

The vibrant green colour of these cutlets comes from the spinach in the marinade. Ginger lends a savoury note to the chops and don't skimp on the quantity of green bird's-eye chillies. Baste the chops with my smoked butter for added flavour.

12 lamb cutlets (I get my butcher to French trim them)
1 tsp ground turmeric
2 tbsp malt vinegar
salt, to taste
smoked butter (page 147), for basting
chaat masala, to garnish
ground ginger, to garnish

### For the marinade

2 tbsp Greek yoghurt
2 tsp chickpea (gram) flour
70 g (2½ oz) spinach leaves
2 tbsp roughly chopped coriander (cilantro)
3 green bird's-eye chillies
2 garlic cloves, roughly chopped
5 cm (2 in) ginger root, roughly chopped
1 tsp sugar

Put the lamb cutlets on a large platter and sprinkle over the turmeric and vinegar. Mix well and set aside while you make the marinade.

Place 1 tablespoon of the yoghurt and the chickpea (gram) flour in a large mixing bowl, mix well and set aside.

Put the remaining yoghurt, spinach, coriander (cilantro), green chillies, garlic, ginger and sugar in a blender and blend to a smooth mix. Do not add any water, the yoghurt will suffice. Add this paste to the bowl with the yoghurt and flour mixture. Season to taste and mix well. Add the cutlets to the bowl and leave to marinate for 2–3 hours, or preferably overnight.

Preheat the oven to 200°C fan (425°F/gas 7). Line a baking tray with foil and place a wire rack over the tray.

Place the cutlets on the wire rack. Place the tray in the oven and cook for 20–25 minutes. Halfway through the cooking time, baste the meat with the smoked butter. Take the cutlets out of the oven and sprinkle over chaat masala and ground ginger while they are still warm.

Serve the lamb cutlets with salad and roti.

# Stir-Fried Lamb with Garlic Green Chilli & Garam Masala

## TAWE KA TIKKA

If you have ever visited Amritsar, Punjab, then you will certainly have eaten this delicious dish. Chunks of lamb are cooked with the warm flavours of cinnamon, cloves and black cardamom (all my favourites!) in a rich yoghurt mixture that clings to the lamb. The two-step cooking process is a must for a tawe ka tikka: the tikkas are braised in the wet marinade before frying in dry ground spices, which create a wonderful smoky aroma. Shoulder of lamb has enough fat that renders as the meat cooks. If necessary, meat tenderizer helps to soften the lamb, but you can swap it for raw papaya purée if you prefer.

5 garlic cloves
3 cm (1 in) ginger root
2 tbsp Greek yoghurt
2 tsp meat tenderizer
1 tsp Kashmiri chilli powder
700 g (1 lb 8¾ oz) boneless shoulder of lamb, cut into 2.5 cm (1 in) chunks

### For frying the tikka

2 tbsp ghee
220 g (7¾ oz) white onions, finely chopped
120 g (4¼ oz) tomatoes, finely chopped
salt, to taste
3 green bird's-eye chillies, slit lengthwise
2 tbsp finely chopped coriander (cilantro) leaves
juice of ½ lemon

### For the garam masala

1 tsp cumin seeds, coarsely crushed
1 tsp ground cinnamon
½ tsp black cardamom powder
1 tsp ground cloves

Grind the garlic and ginger to a paste in a blender with a splash of water. In a bowl, mix the yoghurt, meat tenderizer, garlic and ginger paste with the chilli powder. Stir well and add the lamb chunks to the yoghurt mixture. Coat the pieces and leave to marinate in the fridge for 4–5 hours, or preferably overnight.

Mix together all the ingredients for the garam masala in a small bowl and set aside.

Heat a large saucepan over a medium heat. Add the marinated lamb to the pan without any oil. Cook the lamb, stirring often as the moisture dries out, for 25 minutes. Turn off the heat, cover the pan with the lid and set aside.

When ready to fry the tikka, heat a large tawa or frying pan (skillet) over a medium heat. Add the ghee and then the onions and fry for 18–20 minutes until brown. Stir well and add the tomatoes. Continue frying for 5 minutes as the tomatoes soften and go mushy. Add the cooked lamb to the pan along with the garam masala blend. Season to taste, then add the green chillies. Turn down the heat to low and fry for 5–6 minutes, stirring well, then turn off the heat. Garnish with chopped coriander (cilantro) and lemon juice.

Serve the lamb as a snack or alongside some flatbread and a zingy salad.

# Fried Beef Kebabs with Green Chilli, Coriander & Dried Pomegranate

## CHAPPALI KEBAB

As much as this chapter focusses on lamb, this recipe, which includes beef, has been one of my favourites and I was keen to share it with you all. Originally hailing from Peshawar, you will find a version of this delicious beef kebab at most dhabbas, with kebabwallas selling them piping hot with naan and chutney. The original kebabs were made the size of a slipper — or as we call it, 'chappal' — and that is where the name 'chappali' comes from. Along with the spices, the quality of the meat used is what gives it the wonderful texture. Grinding the beef a few times is necessary to achieve a smooth mixture. Remember, once you have added all the spices, make sure to knead the minced (ground) beef well, just like you would dough. It's also important to use beef with a high fat content, which will hold together well and give loads of flavour. This kebab is rich, robust and totally unapologetic.

2 eggs
600 g (1 lb 5 oz) minced (ground) beef (I opt for chuck steak with a good amount of fat)
4 green bird's-eye chillies, ground to a paste
7.5 cm (3 in) ginger root, roughly chopped and ground to a paste
70 g (2½ oz) onions, finely chopped
60 g (2 oz) tomatoes, seeds removed and finely chopped
1 tbsp coriander seeds, coarsely crushed
1 tsp Kashmiri chilli powder
2 heaped tbsp pomegranate powder
2 tbsp finely chopped fresh coriander (cilantro)
2 tbsp chickpea (gram) flour
2–3 tbsp vegetable oil
salt, to taste

Whisk 1 of the eggs in a bowl and then scramble in a small pan until firm. Set aside.

In a large mixing bowl, add the minced (ground) beef along with the green chilli and ginger pastes, onions, tomato, coriander seeds, chilli powder, pomegranate powder and chopped coriander (cilantro). Whisk the remaining egg and add to the bowl along with the scrambled egg. Season to taste.

Add the chickpea (gram) flour and knead the mixture for 6–7 minutes. It's important to mix everything well until the chappali kebab mixture goes smooth and all the ingredients blend together. Cover and leave to rest in the fridge for a few hours, or overnight.

Heat 1 tablespoon of the oil in a large non-stick frying pan (skillet) over a medium heat. Divide the mixture into 6 equal portions. Flatten each kebab into a 15–18 cm (6–7 in) round. Working in batches, add the chappali kebabs to the pan, flatten them slightly and cook for 4–5 minutes on each side until they go crispy around the edges and are cooked through. Remove from the pan and drain on kitchen paper.

Serve warm with naan and chutney of your choice.

# Lamb Kebabs with Cardamom, Chilli & Mint

## SHAMI KEBAB

The many kebabs I have eaten at stalls and night markets across streets of Mumbai, Pune, Delhi, Hyderabad and Lucknow all provide the inspiration for the kebabs I now cook at home. Taking its influence from Awadhi cooking (mainly from the Nawab Wazir of Oudh in the eighteenth century), these shami kebabs include spices and chillies that were part of the Maratha influence. They are cooked over a large pan and fried until golden brown. My first taste of them came at a little Mughlai cafe in Tardeo, Mumbai, who served the most delicious shami kebabs when I was younger. I was keen to celebrate and share what I know is such a popular dish, not just at street stalls but also in restaurants and homes.

### For the kebab mixture

500 g (1 lb 1½ oz) minced
    (ground) leg of lamb (you can
    use beef, if you prefer)
100 g (3½ oz) chana dal,
    soaked in water overnight
    and then drained
50 g (1¾ oz) red onion,
    roughly chopped
5 garlic cloves, roughly chopped
5 cm (2 in) ginger root,
    roughly chopped
2 dried Kashmiri chillies
1 tsp cumin seeds
2 dried bay leaves
2 mace blades
4 green cardamom pods
    (seeds only)
salt, to taste

### For the kebabs

1 egg
4 tbsp chopped mint leaves
3 green bird's-eye chillies,
    finely chopped
2 tsp dried mango powder
1 tsp garam masala
ghee or vegetable oil,
    for shallow frying
Spicy Green Chilli Chutney
    (page 136), to serve

Put all the kebab mixture ingredients in a large saucepan, season to taste and add 100 ml (3½ fl oz/scant ½ cup) of water. Cook over a medium heat covered with a lid for 30 minutes, stirring halfway through. Now take the lid off to let all the moisture evaporate so the kebab mixture is as dry as possible — depending on how much moisture your meat contains, this should take no more than 8–10 minutes. Set aside to cool completely.

Working in batches, add this kebab mixture to a mixer grinder or food processor and grind to a smooth mix. This might take some time as you will need to scrape down the sides of the mixer as you blend.

Place the smooth kebab mixture in a large mixing bowl along with the egg, mint, green chillies, mango powder and garam masala. Mix well and divide the shami kebab mixture into 12 equal portions. Roll each portion into a ball and then flatten each one slightly.

Heat the ghee or oil in a large frying pan (skillet) over a medium heat. Don't add too much ghee or oil as you want the shami kebabs to hold their shape as they fry. Working in batches, fry the kebabs for 1–2 minutes on each side until they go crispy and golden brown. Drain on kitchen pepper.

Serve the kebabs warm with Spicy Green Chilli Chutney.

# Spiced Lamb Skewers with Black Pepper, Cumin & Dried Mango

## KANDAHARI GOSHT TIKKA

Adding sour notes to tandoori cooking is a classic north Indian technique, which has made its way out of the region of Kandahar. This recipe uses dried mango powder to supply that sour note. For these lamb skewers, I include some additional lamb fat to the meat which renders as it grills to give lots more flavour. Ask your butcher for some extra fat diced into small pieces. Marinated in yoghurt with crushed black pepper, cumin seeds and garam masala, these tikka are tangy, spicy and so, so good.

You will need wooden skewers
    soaked in cold water for
    30 minutes

3 garlic cloves, roughly chopped
3 cm (1 in) ginger root,
    roughly chopped
1 heaped tbsp Greek yoghurt
½ tsp coarsely crushed
    black pepper
1 tsp coarsely crushed cumin seeds
1 heaped tsp garam masala
1 tsp meat tenderizer (optional)
650 g (1 lb 7 oz) lamb rump,
    cut into bite-size pieces
2 tsp dried mango powder,
    to garnish
sea salt, to garnish
smoked butter (page 147),
    for basting

Pound the garlic and ginger to a paste in a blender with a splash of water. Put the garlic and ginger paste, yoghurt, pepper, cumin and garam masala in a mixing bowl. Add the meat tenderizer, if using. Stir well and add the lamb (along with the lamb fat, if using) to the bowl. Do not add any salt at this stage — you can season the kebabs sparingly once cooked. Stir well and leave to marinate in the fridge for 6–8 hours.

Mix together the mango powder and salt in a small bowl and set aside.

Thread the lamb and lamb fat onto the soaked wooden skewers. Heat a griddle pan over a medium heat and cook the Kandahari tikka for 4 minutes. Baste the skewers with the smoked butter and turn over, then cook the tikka for a further 4 minutes.

Serve the Kandahari tikka warm with a sprinkle of the mango powder mix.

# Slow-Roasted Leg of Lamb with Ginger, Cardamom, Cloves & Saffron

## RAAN MUSALLAM

I cannot write a recipe book on tandoori cooking without including raan! This slow-roasted leg of lamb, with its influences in flavours and cooking style from Peshawar and the British Raj, traditionally follows a two-step marination process. The meat is tenderized before being cooked slowly over hot coals and then finished in a tandoor for a wonderful charred flavour. One of my fondest memories of eating raan has to be at Bukhara in ITC, Delhi, where their closely guarded recipe has impressed diners for years. My recipe for raan includes covering the meat with a dry rub of cardamom, cloves, mace and fennel seeds before marinating it in yoghurt blended with onion, garlic, ginger, saffron and chilli. The lengthy cooking time ensures the tender lamb melts in the mouth and has maximum flavour. Don't skimp on the garnishes served alongside as they give the meal so much more depth.

1.2 kg (2 lb 10¼ oz) leg of lamb
200 ml (6¾ fl oz/¾ cup) warm water

### For the dry marinade

10 green cardamom pods (seeds only)
6 cloves
2 mace blades
4 dried bay leaves
2 tbsp fennel seeds
5 cm (2 in) cinnamon stick

### For the wet marinade

2 tbsp vegetable oil or ghee
150 g (5¼ oz) white onion, thinly sliced
6–7 garlic cloves, roughly chopped
5 cm (2 in) ginger root, roughly chopped
1 green bird's-eye chilli
280 g (10 oz) Greek yoghurt
1½ tsp Kashmiri chilli powder
generous pinch of saffron strands
2 tsp meat tenderizer
salt, to taste

### To serve

½ tsp ground cumin
pinch of black salt
1 tsp dried mango powder
handful of chopped mint leaves
2 tbsp pomegranate seeds

Mix the ground cumin, black salt and mango powder in a small bowl and set aside.

Toast the dry marinade ingredients in a frying pan (skillet) over a low heat for 7–8 minutes. Shake the pan a few times to make sure they toast evenly. Cool and grind to a fine powder. Make a few cuts in the lamb and place in a large deep baking dish. Rub the dry marinade all over the lamb. Leave to marinate for 35–40 minutes while you make the wet marinade.

Heat the oil in a frying pan over a medium heat. Fry the onions for 6–8 minutes until they begin to colour. Add the garlic and ginger continuing to fry for 4 minutes. Stir well and cool this mix. Add this to a grinder along with the green chilli and 2 tablespoons of the yoghurt and blend to a smooth paste. Add to a bowl along with the remaining yoghurt, chilli powder, saffron and meat tenderizer. Season to taste. Pour this marinade over the leg of lamb spreading it evenly across the meat. Cover and marinate in the fridge for 5–6 hours, or preferably overnight.

Take the lamb out of the fridge and leave at room temperature for an hour before cooking.

Preheat the oven to 180°C fan (400°F/gas 6). Place the lamb in a roasting tray, adding the warm water to the base of the tray. Cover in foil and roast in the hot oven for 2 hours, basting halfway through the cooking time. Now take the foil off and roast for a further 25–30 minutes. Take the tray out of the oven, transfer the lamb to a plate and cover. Leave to rest for 20 minutes. Use the remaining juices in the base of the tray to make a gravy, if you prefer.

Carve the lamb into thin slices and garnish with the ground cumin, black salt and dried mango powder. Top with the fresh mint and pomegranate seeds, then serve with mint raita and Khamiri roti.

# FISH & SEAFOOD

My affinity with seafood definitely comes from growing up in the west of India, where coastal ingredients are in abundance and the variety of spices added to seafood is mesmerizing. As a family we ate everything. When I think back, it's those formative years that have left a lasting impression on my cooking. Even today, shopping at my local fishmongers and coming back with a bounty of seafood is typically the most joyous part of my weekend! Being able to adapt recipes using native fish with Indian spices is one of the things I am truly proud of. For the recipes in this chapter I have opted for firm fish that soaks up the marinade and spices but also holds its own once cooked. The trick is understanding the variety of fish to use so that it won't just flake, like the salmon chunks in a basil and coriander (cilantro) marinade used for the Haraa Bharaa Fish Tikka (page 68). Grilling on a high setting keeps both the fish and the marinade intact.

FISH & SEAFOOD

# Salmon Tikka Skewers Marinated in Green Chilli, Basil & Coriander

## HARAA BHARAA FISH TIKKA

As a firm oily fish, salmon soaks up all the goodness of spices really well. This green marinade is unlike any other. The original recipe was shared by Sunaina Khatri, who I met during my visit to Ahmedabad years back. Her family hail from the Gujarati Muslim community who are renowned for making some of the finest biryanis, kebabs and tikkas. The recipe includes Indian basil which isn't readily available, so swapping it for regular basil and fresh coriander (cilantro) has been a revelation. The marinade coats the pink-coloured salmon chunks and is so delicious served with a relish or dip.

3 garlic cloves
3 cm (1 in) ginger root
juice of ½ lime
½ tsp coarsely crushed
　black pepper
2 tbsp vegetable oil
500 g (1 lb 2 oz) skinless
　salmon fillets, cut into
　4 cm (1½ in) chunks
dried mango powder, to garnish

### For the marinade

60 g (2 oz) basil, roughly
　chopped
50 g (1¾ oz) coriander (cilantro),
　roughly chopped
2 green bird's-eye chillies
1 garlic clove, roughly chopped
½ tsp garam masala
2 tbsp Greek yoghurt
salt, to taste

Pound the ginger and garlic together in a pestle and mortar to form a coarse paste. Put the paste in a large mixing bowl along with the lime juice, black pepper and oil. Add the salmon pieces and set aside while you prepare the marinade.

To make the marinade, put the basil, coriander (cilantro), green chillies and garlic in a blender along with the garam masala, yoghurt and salt. Blitz to a smooth paste. Tip the marinade into the bowl with the salmon pieces and leave to marinate for 15–20 minutes.

Preheat the grill (broiler) to a medium-high heat. Line a baking tray with foil and place a wire rack over the tray.

Place the marinated salmon on the wire rack. Grill for 10–12 minutes or until just cooked through. Halfway through the cooking time, baste the salmon with any leftover marinade. Sprinkle with the dried mango powder.

Serve the fish tikka with salad or wrapped in naan or roti.

# Tandoori Masala Fish

An oven-roasted whole fish is coated in a classic tandoori marinade. Traditionally in India this would be done with a local flat fish, like pomfret, however I have used sea bream here, which is a firm, flat fish that cooks really well with spices. The creamy, tandoori marinade forms a crust around the fish that encases the flesh, retaining the moisture and keeping the fish intact.

2 whole sea bream (about 280 g/
   10 oz each), scaled and gutted
1 tsp ground turmeric
2 tbsp lemon juice
pinch of salt
smoked butter (page 147)
   or ghee, for basting
grilled lemons (page 142),
   to serve

### For the marinade

3 garlic cloves
3 cm (1 in) ginger root
50 g (1¾ oz) cashew nuts,
   soaked in hot water for
   20 minutes
2 tbsp Greek yoghurt
1 heaped tsp chickpea (gram)
   flour
1 tbsp vegetable oil
1 tsp Kashmiri chilli powder
½ tsp ground white pepper
1 tbsp ground coriander
2 tbsp chopped coriander
   (cilantro) leaves
salt, to taste

Lay the sea bream on a large plate. Sprinkle the turmeric, lemon juice and salt over the fish and rub it into the skin. Set aside while you make the marinade.

Pound the garlic and ginger to a paste in a pestle and mortar and set aside.

Blend the cashew nuts with 7 tablespoons of water to a smooth, fine paste. Place in a large bowl along with the yoghurt, flour, oil and garlic and ginger paste. Add the chilli powder, pepper, ground coriander and season to taste. Add the coriander (cilantro) leaves and stir well. Spread this marinade all over the fish and leave to marinate for 1 hour.

Preheat the oven to 210°C fan (450°F/gas 8). Line a baking tray with with foil and place a wire rack over the tray.

Place the marinated tandoori fish on the wire rack and bake in the hot oven for 20–25 minutes. Halfway through the cooking time, baste the fish with the smoked butter. Once the flesh is cooked through and the marinade has formed a crust, transfer the fish to a serving platter.

Serve the fish warm with the grilled lemons, naan, chutney and salad.

# Tandoori Fish Tikka with Turmeric, Carom Seeds & Chaat Masala

## AJWAIN FISH TIKKA

Carom seeds are one of my favourite spices and with a hint of pungency work really well in flatbreads, stir fries and are commonly added to fish as well. This fish tikka is marinated in yoghurt with crushed carom seeds, turmeric and mustard oil. A true Punjabi recipe and one that is quick to cook.

650 g (1 lb 7 oz) cod loin, cut into bite-size pieces
ghee, for basting
chaat masala, to finish

### For the first marinade

3 garlic cloves
3 cm (1 in) ginger root
½ tsp Kashmiri chilli powder
½ tsp ground turmeric
pinch of salt

### For the second marinade

3 tbsp Greek yoghurt
1 heaped tsp chickpea (gram) flour
1 tsp carom seeds (*ajwain*)
½ tsp Kashmiri chilli powder
1 tbsp mustard oil
½ tsp garam masala
salt, to taste

Lay the cod pieces on a large plate. Pound the garlic and ginger to a paste in a pestle and mortar. Mix this paste with all the other first marinade ingredients in a bowl and spread it over the cod pieces. Set aside while you make the second marinade.

To make the second marinade, mix together the yoghurt and chickpea (gram) flour in a bowl until smooth. Combine with all the remaining second marinade ingredients, season to taste and then spread this marinade all over the fish. Set aside to marinate for 15–20 minutes.

Preheat the grill (broiler) to a high heat. Line a baking tray with foil.

Place the fish tikka on the tray and grill for 4 minutes. Baste the cod pieces with the ghee and grill for a further 4 minutes. Serve the ajwain fish tikka with a generous sprinkle of chaat masala.

# Whole Roasted Sea Bream with Black Pepper, Curry Leaves, Tamarind & Chilli

## FISH POLLICHATHU

Travelling through Kerala you'll spot lots of toddy shops along the way and this stuffed fish dish is usually on the menu. The classic recipe uses a local fish known as karimeen, which is pan-fried in a banana leaf over a wood fire. The spice mix usually includes an ingredient known as kodampuli, which gives the paste its tangy, sour flavour. For my recipe, I have used sea bream — a firm white flat fish that is locally available in the UK — wrapping the whole fish in a banana leaf and baking it in the oven, although you can use parchment paper if you can't find banana leaves. Tamarind pastes can vary in strength so be sure to check its flavour before adding and adjust accordingly.

2 whole sea bream or any
    medium white flat fish
    (about 300 g/10½ oz each),
    scaled and gutted
2 banana leaves

### For the marinade

1 tsp ground turmeric
juice of ½ lemon
pinch of salt

### For the masala

3 tbsp coconut oil
300 g (10½ oz) white onions,
    thinly sliced
10–12 curry leaves
6 garlic cloves, finely chopped
5 cm (2 in) ginger root,
    finely chopped
1½ tsp Kashmiri chilli powder
1 tbsp ground coriander
¼ tsp ground black pepper
2 tsp tamarind paste
salt, to taste
pinch of sugar

Place the sea bream on a large plate. Make a few cuts in the fish and sprinkle over the turmeric, lemon juice and a little salt. Set aside to marinate while you make the masala.

Heat the oil for the masala in a large frying pan (skillet) over a medium heat. Add the onions along with half the curry leaves and fry for 17–18 minutes. They will begin to soften and change colour. Add the chopped garlic and ginger and fry for 2 minutes. At this stage, add the chilli powder, ground coriander and pepper. Stir well and add the tamarind paste along with 50 ml (1¾ fl oz/¼ cup) of water. Turn off the heat. Season to taste and add the sugar. Mix well and leave to cool.

Preheat the oven to 200°C fan (425°F/gas 7). If you are using banana leaves, hold them just above an open flame to make them easier to fold. Add a little oil to the non-shiny side of the banana leaf.

Spoon a quarter of the masala onto the banana leaf or piece of parchment paper, place the fish on it and top with another quarter of the masala. Repeat this for the second sea bream. Wrap the fish in the banana leaf or parchment paper to make a neat, sealed parcel — fold the sides inwards and, if necessary, secure the parcel with a wooden skewer or toothpick. Once sealed, place the parcels on a roasting tray. Roast in the hot oven for 20 minutes. When ready to serve, open up the parcels to reveal the fish.

*See photos on pages 74–5.*

Whole Roasted Sea Bream with Black Pepper,
Curry Leaves, Tamarind & Chilli

# Ginger–Marinated King Prawns with Turmeric, Mustard & Chilli

### ADRAKI TANDOORI JHINGE

Grilling prawns brings me so much joy, especially when they are coated in this simple marinade. My recipe includes mustard oil in the marinade — a pungent vibrant oil that lends a savoury note to balance the sweetness of the prawns. Even though it's just a tablespoon, it works really well. If you cannot get hold of mustard oil, you can swap it for half a teaspoon of English mustard, which will equally lend that savoury edge. For a perfect midweek meal, grill the prawns on a high heat until they are charred around the edges and serve just with some flatbread, pickled onions, chutney and salad.

12–15 king prawns, deveined
    and tails left on
smoked butter (page 147)
    or ghee, for basting

**For the marinade**

3 tbsp Greek yoghurt
2 tsp chickpea (gram) flour
5 cm (2 in) ginger root,
    finely grated (shredded)
1 tbsp mustard oil
1 tsp ground turmeric
½ tsp Kashmiri chilli powder
2 tsp ground ginger
salt, to taste

Combine all the marinade ingredients in a large bowl. Mix well and season to taste. Add the prawns to the bowl and set aside to marinate for 30 minutes.

Preheat the grill (broiler) to a high heat. Line a baking tray with foil and place a wire rack over the tray.

Brush the wire rack with butter or ghee. Place the prawns on the wire rack. Grill for 4 minutes, baste with smoked butter or ghee and grill for a further 4 minutes until they are lightly charred and cooked through.

Serve warm with parathas or rotis, pickled onions, salad and my Spicy Green Chilli Chutney.

# Spicy Goan Prawns with Garlic, Chilli & Tamarind

## RECHEADO JHINGE

Although this recheado is commonly made using pan-fried fish, it works really well with grilled prawns too. This classic masala base from the state of Goa balances the sweetness of the prawns, which I have cooked in a griddle pan to lend them a wonderful smoky flavour. Make sure you use large tiger prawns and fully coat them in the thick chilli paste. I butterfly the prawns and then fill the cavities with the paste to ensure that they take on maximum flavour while they cook. If you have any left over, this chilli paste freezes well.

10 dried Kashmiri chillies, deseeded
12 tiger prawns, shell and head left on
6 cloves
½ tsp cumin seeds
½ tsp black peppercorns
pinch of ground cinnamon
6–8 garlic cloves, roughly chopped
3 cm (1 in) ginger root, roughly chopped
3 tbsp dark soft brown sugar
2 tbsp malt vinegar
1 tbsp tamarind paste
salt, to taste
2 tsp fish sauce

Soak the dried chillies in a bowl of hot water and set aside for 20 minutes.

Using kitchen scissors, cut through the shell of each prawn from just below the head to the tail following the line of its back. Devein the prawns by removing the line that runs down each prawn with your fingers. Leaving the shells on, butterfly the prawns by slicing part way only through each prawn to create a cavity that will later be filled with the paste. Set aside on a plate while you make the paste.

Put the soaked chillies in a blender with 50 ml (1¾ fl oz/ ¼ cup) of their soaking liquid. Add the cloves, cumin, black peppercorns, cinnamon, garlic, ginger, sugar, vinegar and tamarind paste, then blend to a smooth paste. Decant into a bowl, season to taste and add the fish sauce. Stir well.

Spread this paste over each prawn, including inside the butterflied cavity.

Heat a griddle pan over a medium flame, add the prawns a few at a time and cook for 2–3 minutes on each side until lightly charred and cooked through.

Serve warm with roti, salad and my Tangy Chilli & Coriander Dipping Sauce.

# VEGETARIAN

The recipes in this chapter are the ones I cook most often in my own kitchen. Using vegetables as the centrepiece of a meal provides versatility throughout the week. There is also the advantage that grilling or roasting vegetables is not a long, drawn-out cooking process. The marinades included here are simple and delicious, lending flavour to paneer, cauliflower, sweetcorn, bell peppers and potatoes. Whenever I have a busy week, I always keep a packet of paneer and a couple of aubergines (eggplants) in the fridge — both are great for soaking up spicy marinades and take only minutes to grill. Sundays are for roasting a whole cauliflower with coconut milk and saffron (Gobi Tandoori, page 94), similar to an Awadhi korma. Two of my favourite vegetarian recipes are the tandoori potatoes soaked in a buttermilk marinade (Tandoori Aloo Chaat, page 88) and, of course, the chargrilled sweetcorn with a chilli-spiked butter (Makkai Butta, page 92), which brings back memories of corn-on-the-cobs cooked over coals on rainy monsoon days in Mumbai.

VEGETARIAN

# Spicy Potato & Fig Cakes
# with Chilli, Mint & Coriander

**ALOO AUR ANJEER KI TIKKI**

Using dried fruit and nuts in snacks and starters has always been a key part of the Awadhi cuisine. This isn't just a simple spiced potato cake; it's stuffed with a filling of dried figs, ginger, chilli, mint and coriander (cilantro). The sweet and savoury stuffing gives not only flavour but also texture, and provides a little surprise when you bite into the cake. This potato mixture is usually shaped like a kebab to cook in a tandoor, however I prefer to shape them into round patties.

500 g (1 lb 1½ oz) potatoes, boiled, cooled and peeled
1 tsp cumin seeds
1 tsp Kashmiri chilli powder
1 tbsp ground coriander
1 tbsp finely chopped mint leaves
1 tbsp finely chopped coriander (cilantro) leaves
2 tbsp dried breadcrumbs
salt, to taste
oil, for shallow frying

### For the filling

7 dried figs, finely chopped
3 tbsp mascarpone
1 tsp ground coriander
2.5 cm (1 in) ginger root, finely chopped
1 green bird's-eye chilli, finely chopped (add a little more if you prefer it spicy)
2 tsp dried mango powder
1 tbsp finely chopped coriander (cilantro) leaves

Mix together all the filling ingredients in a small bowl. Chill in the fridge for 20 minutes.

Coarsely grate (shred) the potatoes into a large mixing bowl. Add the cumin seeds, chilli powder, ground coriander, mint leaves, coriander (cilantro) leaves, breadcrumbs and salt, mix well and then divide the mixture into 8 patties or tikkis.

Working with one portion at a time, make a small well in a tikki and add ½ tablespoon of the fig filling. Bring the tikki up from all sides to enclose the filling, making sure it stays in the middle and so will not leak out.

Heat the oil for shallow frying in a large, non-stick frying pan (skillet) over a medium heat. Working in batches, add the aloo tikki to the hot pan and fry for 2–3 minutes on each side until golden brown and crispy. Drain on kitchen paper before serving. Serve with a fresh chutney.

# Potato, Paneer & Sweetcorn Kebabs

SERVES 4

## SUBZ SEEKH

Seekh kebabs are such a popular item on the menus of grilled dishes at street stalls and restaurants. This vegetarian version of the seekh kebab is one of my absolute favourites and is equally as delicious as any meat kebab. Sweetcorn, carrots, potato and paneer are combined with a classic kebab masala, including cardamom, black pepper and dried mango powder. I have cooked these kebabs in a griddle pan, although you can also shallow fry them until they are evenly golden all over.

2 tbsp vegetable oil, plus extra for grilling
1 tsp cumin seeds
5 cm (2 in) ginger root, finely chopped
2 green bird's-eye chillies, finely chopped
120 g (4½ oz) carrots, peeled and finely diced
150 g (5¼ oz) canned, drained sweetcorn
1 tbsp ground coriander
½ tsp garam masala
150 g (5¼ oz) potato, peeled, boiled, cooled and coarsely grated (shredded)
70 g (2½ oz) paneer, finely grated (shredded)
1 heaped tsp dried mango powder
1 tsp ground cardamom
1 tbsp finely chopped coriander (cilantro) leaves
2 tbsp finely chopped mint leaves
2 tbsp chickpea (gram) flour
1 tbsp breadcrumbs
salt, to taste

Heat the 2 tablespoons of vegetable oil in a large frying pan (skillet) over a medium heat. Add the cumin seeds and, as they begin to splutter, add the ginger and fry for 30 seconds, then add the green chillies. Stir well, add the carrots and cook for 4–5 minutes. Add the sweetcorn, stir well and fry for 2 minutes. Add the ground coriander and garam masala, turn off the heat and leave to cool completely.

Once cool, blend the carrot and sweetcorn mixture in a blender to a coarse, dry mix — do not add any water. Transfer to a large mixing bowl and add the grated (shredded) potato, paneer, dried mango powder, ground cardamom, coriander (cilantro) leaves and mint leaves. Season to taste and add the chickpea (gram) flour along with the breadcrumbs. Mix well. Shape into 6 sausages and chill in the fridge for 20 minutes.

Heat a griddle pan over a high heat. Lightly brush the kebabs with a little oil. Cook the subz seekh in the hot pan for 2 minutes on each side until lightly charred and evenly browned all over.

Serve with roti, green chutney and salad.

# Buttermilk Tandoori Potatoes with Green Chilli, Cumin & Chaat Masala

## TANDOORI ALOO CHAAT

Tandoori aloo has such a unique flavour. The potatoes are commonly roasted in a spicy dressing and are sometimes even stuffed before being grilled. The dressing is so thick that it clings to the potatoes, ensuring that they are evenly cooked and coated in all the spices. In Delhi, the ITC Bukhara restaurant serve an excellent tandoori aloo with the perfect ratio of dressing to the size of potatoes so that the dish is never dry or bland. I prefer to use small baby potatoes, roasted until light brown and tossed in a creamy, tangy buttermilk mixture spiked with green chillies and garam masala, then finished with chaat masala and mint leaves.

700 g (1 lb 8¾ oz) baby potatoes
3 tbsp vegetable oil
2 garlic cloves, finely grated (shredded)
salt, to taste
pinch of chaat masala
handful of mint leaves, chopped

### For the dressing

3 green bird's-eye chillies, roughly chopped
½ tsp cumin seeds, coarsely crushed
300 ml (10 fl oz/1¼ cups) buttermilk
2 tsp chickpea (gram) flour
½ tsp garam masala

Preheat the oven to 220°C fan (475°F/gas 9).

Put the potatoes in a roasting tray and add the oil, garlic and salt. Stir well and roast in the hot oven for 15 minutes.

Meanwhile, make the dressing. In a pestle and mortar, crush the green chillies and cumin seeds to a rough paste and transfer to a mixing bowl. Add the buttermilk and chickpea (gram) flour, then stir well to get rid of any lumps. Stir in the garam masala.

Remove the potatoes from the oven and pour over buttermilk dressing. Stir well, making sure all the potatoes are coated in the mixture. Return the potatoes to the oven for a further 15 minutes, stirring halfway through the cooking time.

Serve the tandoori aloo warm with a pinch of chaat masala and fresh mint leaves.

# Aubergine Tikkas in Creamy Yoghurt, Mustard, Chilli & Ginger

## TANDOORI BAINGAN

Aubergine (eggplant) and onion pieces are marinated in a spiced, creamy yoghurt before being chargrilled. Aubergine retains its shape when grilled, but I do find that during cooking much of the marinade tends to dry out and so basting the kebabs with butter is essential to retain moisture. The best way to amplify flavour in this kebab is to divide the marinade and the reserved half to coat the chunks of aubergine and onion once cooked; this way the aroma and taste from the creamy yoghurt marinade remain intact.

You will need wooden skewers soaked in cold water for 30 minutes

400 g (14 oz) aubergines (eggplants), quartered and cut into large chunks
200 g (7 oz) red onions, quartered
melted butter, for basting
generous pinch of chaat masala
pinch of garam masala

### For the marinade

4 garlic cloves
5 cm (2 in) ginger root
2 green bird's-eye chillies
8 tbsp Greek yoghurt
1 tsp Kashmiri chilli powder
1½ tsp ground coriander
1 tsp ground turmeric
1 tbsp mustard oil
1 tbsp dried fenugreek leaves (*kasoori methi*), crushed
pinch of sugar
salt, to taste

To make the marinade, blend the garlic, ginger and green chillies with a splash of water in a blender. Put the paste in a large mixing bowl along with the yoghurt, chilli powder, ground coriander and turmeric. Add the mustard oil, fenugreek leaves and sugar, then season to taste. Stir well.

Set aside half the marinade in a separate bowl. Add the chunks of aubergine (eggplant) and red onion to the marinade in the large mixing bowl. Mix well to make sure each piece is fully coated in the marinade. Set aside for 1 hour.

Meanwhile, tip the reserved marinade into a non-stick frying pan (skillet). Cook over a medium heat for 6–7 minutes, stirring continuously to make sure it doesn't stick to the bottom of the pan, until the marinade thickens and changes colour slightly. Transfer this marinade to a mixing bowl, cover and set aside.

Preheat the grill (broiler) to a medium heat. Line a baking tray with foil and place a wire rack over the tray.

Thread the aubergine pieces onto the soaked wooden skewers, alternating them with the onion pieces. Place the skewers on the wire rack and grill for 7–8 minutes. Take the tray out from under the grill, baste with the butter, put it back under the grill and cook for a further 6–7 minutes until lightly charred and cooked through.

Add the grilled aubergines and onions to the bowl with the cooked marinade. Add a generous pinch of chaat masala and small pinch of garam masala before serving.

Serve warm with roti and chutney.

*See photos on pages 90–1.*

Aubergine Tikkas in Creamy Yoghurt, Mustard, Chilli & Ginger

# Chargrilled Corn-on-the-Cob with Chilli & Lime Butter

## MAKKAI BUTTA

I will never stop loving the chargrilled corn-on-the-cobs served across the streets of Mumbai. I hold special memories of eating them in the pouring rain during the monsoon season. For this recipe, which is hard to resist, I have taken the very same flavours of those cobs of sweetcorn cooked over coals and brought them into my home kitchen. Cooking the sweetcorn directly over an open flame gives it that lovely smoky flavour, although if you prefer you can also use a griddle pan. I usually make double the amount of spiced butter and store it in the freezer for the next time I cook makkai butta.

4 corn-on-the-cobs
juice of 2 limes

### For the spiced butter

5 tbsp melted butter
1 tsp Kashmiri chilli powder
zest of 2 limes
handful of coriander (cilantro)
   leaves, finely chopped
generous pinch of salt

To make the spiced butter, combine the melted butter, chilli powder, lime zest, chopped coriander (cilantro) and salt in a bowl. Mix well and set aside.

Taking care, cook the corn-on-the-cobs over an open flame until they are lightly charred all over.

Place the hot sweetcorn on a serving plate and smear some of the spiced butter over each cob. Squeeze over a little lime juice before serving.

# Whole Roasted Cauliflower in a Creamy Coconut & Chilli Sauce

## GOBI TANDOORI

A whole roasted tandoori cauliflower is always the star of the lunch table. Traditionally cauliflower florets are cooked in a tandoor, but for ease of cooking I have marinated a whole cauliflower in spices, including the leaves and stem, and then roasted it in the oven. Taking inspiration from the classic Mughal flavours of a korma, it's cooked in rich coconut milk, which gives a wonderful creamy consistency to the gravy in the bottom of the roasting tin. Basting the cauliflower with the saffron-infused coconut gravy while it cooks ensures the florets are coated in spices.

1 large cauliflower
1 heaped tsp ground turmeric
pinch of salt
800 ml (27 fl oz/3⅓ cups) creamy, full-fat coconut milk
handful of slivered or crushed almonds, to garnish
1 tbsp finely chopped coriander (cilantro) leaves, to garnish

### For the marinade

3 tbsp melted ghee or butter
2 garlic cloves, finely grated (shredded)
5 cm (2 in) ginger root, finely grated (shredded)
1½ tsp Kashmiri chilli powder (or mild chilli powder)
2 tsp ground cumin
½ tsp ground nutmeg
generous pinch of saffron strands
salt, to taste

Trim the excess outer leaves from the cauliflower and cut across its base so that it sits flat.

Pour enough water into a large, deep saucepan to cover the cauliflower. Add the turmeric and a pinch of salt to the water. Bring the water to a boil over a medium heat and then submerge the cauliflower, upside down, in the boiling water and cook for 7–8 minutes. Remove the cauliflower from the pan, drain and set aside for 20 minutes while you prepare the marinade.

In a bowl, combine the melted ghee or butter with the grated (shredded) garlic, ginger, chilli powder, ground cumin, nutmeg and saffron. Season to taste. Place the cauliflower on a plate and cover it in this spiced marinade, coating all the florets, stems and crevices.

Preheat the oven to 200°C fan (425°F/gas 7).

Pour the coconut milk into a deep roasting tin or baking dish and stir in any remaining marinade. Place the cauliflower in the tin and roast in the hot oven for 50 minutes. Halfway through the cooking time, baste the cauliflower with the coconut milk. The coconut milk will reduce and thicken and the cauliflower will cook all the way through.

Serve warm, cut into thick slices or wedges and garnished with the almonds and coriander (cilantro).

# Green Bell Peppers Stuffed with Spicy Potatoes, Chilli & Dried Mango

## TANDOORI SHIMLA MIRCH

When I lived in India my mum would make this recipe often, especially when she had friends over. It's a family favourite that I wanted to share because of my love for green bell peppers. The bell peppers are stuffed with spiced, crushed potatoes that are also flavoured with dried mango powder, which lends that tangy, sour note. The bell peppers we used to get in India were much smaller than those found here in the UK, so when we cooked them at home we would cut the tops off, stuff them and then grill them or sit them over a pan to cook. Because these are slightly bigger, here I have halved the bell peppers lengthwise and then stuffed and grilled them, which softens the pepper slightly although they still retain some bite.

4 medium green bell peppers, halved lengthwise, stems left on and deseeded
2 tbsp vegetable oil
pinch of salt

### For the filling

2 tbsp vegetable oil
pinch of asafoetida
1 tsp cumin seeds
2 green bird's-eye chillies, finely chopped
1 heaped tsp ground coriander
1 tsp ground turmeric
½ tsp Kashmiri chilli powder
600 g (1 lb 5 oz) potatoes, boiled, peeled and lightly crushed
1 tsp dried mango powder
2 tbsp finely chopped coriander (cilantro) leaves
salt, to taste

Brush the inside of each bell pepper with the oil and sprinkle with a little salt. Set aside while you make the filling.

To make the filling, heat the oil in a large non-stick saucepan over a medium heat. Add the asafoetida and cumin seeds and, as they splutter, quickly add the green chillies, ground coriander, turmeric and chilli powder. Add the crushed potatoes and stir well for 1 minute. Lower the heat, season to taste and add the dried mango powder along with chopped coriander (cilantro). Turn off the heat, cover and leave to cool completely.

Divide the potato filling equally between the eight bell pepper halves. Press the filling down into the bell peppers so they are well stuffed.

Heat a griddle pan over a high flame. Brush the top and base of each shimla mirch with oil and place them, potato filling side down, onto the grill and cook for 5–6 minutes. Turn the bell peppers over, so they are now potato filling side up, and grill for a further 8 minutes.

Serve warm with chutney and roti.

# Sweet Potato Chaat with Tamarind Chutney, Pickled Onions & Sev

## SHAKARKANDI CHAAT

The roasted sweet potato gives this chaat a real charred, caramelized sweetness. Topped with zingy chutneys, pickled onions and green chillies, the sweetness of the root vegetable is balanced by the other spicy, tangy flavours in each mouthful. The crispy sev (a delicious deep-fried snack made from chickpea or gram flour) adds a crunchy texture to this colourful chaat recipe.

700 g (1 lb 8½ oz) sweet potato, peeled and cut into 2.5 cm (1 in) pieces
2 tbsp vegetable oil
1 tsp chaat masala

### For the pickled onions

100 g (3½ oz) red onion, finely chopped
7.5 cm (3 in) ginger root, finely chopped
1 green bird's-eye chilli, finely chopped
juice of ½ lime
salt, to taste

### To serve

Spicy Green Chilli Chutney (page 136)
Tangy Tamarind Chutney (page 137)
fresh coriander (cilantro) leaves, finely chopped
handful of sev

Preheat the oven to 200°C fan (425°F/gas 7).

Put all the pickled onion ingredients in a bowl. Stir well and set aside.

Put the sweet potato in a roasting tray, pour over the oil and stir well. Roast in the hot oven for 35 minutes, stirring halfway through the cooking time so they colour evenly.

Once the sweet potato is cooked through and charred around the edges, transfer it to a mixing bowl. Add the chaat masala along with 2 tablespoons of the pickled onions and mix well. Arrange over a large serving platter.

To serve, top the sweet potato with a few tablespoons of the Spicy Green Chilli Chutney along with the Tangy Tamarind Chutney. Add a little more of the pickled onions, some sev and chopped coriander (cilantro). Serve immediately, placing the remaining chutneys, sev and pickled onions on the table in case anyone wants to add a little more.

# Tandoori Spiced Jackfruit with Garlic, Chilli & Coriander

## TANDOORI KATHAL TIKKA

Young jackfruit is used often in Indian recipes, be they curries, stir fries or pan-fried cakes. These tikkas are a perfect vegetable skewer and simple to put together. My recipe uses canned jackfruit and takes only a few moments to cook.

You will need wooden skewers soaked in cold water for 30 minutes

450 g (1 lb) canned jackfruit, drained and rinsed
melted ghee, for basting
juice of 1 lime, to garnish

### For the marinade

4 tbsp Greek yoghurt
2 heaped tsp chickpea (gram) flour
4 garlic cloves, grated (shredded)
½ tsp Kashmiri chilli powder
1 tsp garam masala
2 tsp dried mango powder
salt, to taste
2 tbsp finely chopped coriander (cilantro) leaves

To make the marinade, combine the yoghurt, chickpea (gram) flour, garlic, chilli powder, garam masala and dried mango powder in a bowl. Mix well, season to taste and then stir through the chopped coriander (cilantro). Add the jackfruit chunks to the marinade, making sure they are all fully coated.

Preheat the grill (broiler) to medium-high. Line a baking tray with foil and place a wire rack over the tray.

Thread the marinated jackfruit pieces on the soaked wooden skewers. Place the skewers on the wire rack and top with any leftover marinade. Grill for 6 minutes, turn the skewers, baste with ghee and continue grilling for a further 6 minutes. Squeeze over the lime juice and serve the kathal tikka with naan, chutney and salad.

# Spiced Yoghurt & Paneer Kebabs with Chilli, Ginger & Garam Masala

**DAHI KE KEBAB**

Having eaten these kebabs from a very young age, I have yearned to share the recipe for this dish. Finally, it feels as though I can fully celebrate this meat-free kebab that has been much loved and enthusiastically devoured for years. Rich, thickened, strained yoghurt is mixed with grated (shredded) paneer, spices, ginger and green chillies. Make sure you finely grate the paneer and use strained yoghurt, which ensures that you can shape the mixture into kebabs to cook in a griddle pan or under a hot grill until crispy and golden brown.

250 g (9 oz) Greek yoghurt
120 g (4¼ oz) paneer, finely grated (shredded)
2 tbsp fine breadcrumbs
2 tbsp chickpea (gram) flour
2 tbsp finely chopped coriander (cilantro) leaves
2 green bird's-eye chillies, finely chopped
2.5 cm (1 in) ginger root, finely chopped
½ tsp coarsely crushed cumin seeds
¼ tsp garam masala
salt, to taste
oil, for shallow frying

The day before, put the yoghurt into a clean piece of muslin. Gather up the edges of the muslin and tie them in a knot to secure. Hang the muslin over a kitchen tap (faucet) and leave it there overnight to allow the moisture to drain and the yoghurt to thicken.

In a large mixing bowl, combine the grated (shredded) paneer, breadcrumbs, chickpea (gram) flour, chopped coriander, green chillies, ginger, cumin and garam masala. Unwrap the strained yoghurt and add it to the mixing bowl. Season to taste, stir well to make a thick mixture, then roll into balls about the size of golf balls and flatten slightly. Chill in the fridge for 20 minutes.

Heat the oil for shallow frying in a large, non-stick frying pan (skillet) over a medium heat. Add the kebabs to the pan and fry for 2–3 minutes on each side until light brown and crisp. Drain on kitchen paper before serving.

Serve warm with chutney and salad.

# Saffron–Infused Paneer with Chilli, Ginger and Yoghurt

## ZAFRANI PANEER TIKKA

Saffron-infused paneer is marinated in creamy yoghurt with garlic, ginger, green chillies and spices. Paneer soaks up the flavours of spices really well and also cooks quickly. As well as intensifying the delicious flavour, basting the paneer with saffron butter gives it a vibrant colour. Served with naan and a fresh mint raita, this is one of my absolute favourite grilled paneer recipes.

You will need wooden skewers soaked in cold water for 30 minutes

500 g (1 lb 2 oz) paneer
2 tbsp melted butter, for basting
pinch of saffron strands
250 g (9 oz) green bell pepper, deseeded and cut into cubes
juice of ½ lime
chaat masala, to garnish
mint raita (page 141), to serve

### For the marinade

2 garlic cloves, roughly chopped
1.5 cm (½ in) ginger root, roughly chopped
2 green bird's-eye chillies
5 tbsp Greek yoghurt
2 tsp chickpea (gram) flour
1 tsp ground green cardamom
½ tsp fennel powder
½ tsp saffron strands, lightly crushed
salt, to taste

Cut the paneer into 8 equal cubes and set aside.

Mix the melted butter for basting with the saffron strands and set aside to infuse.

To make the marinade, grind the garlic, ginger and chillies in a blender with a splash of water to a coarse paste and set aside. Put the yoghurt in a large mixing bowl along with the chickpea (gram) flour. Mix well to get rid of any lumps. Add the garlic, ginger and chilli paste to the bowl as well as the ground cardamom, fennel powder and crushed saffron. Season to taste.

Add the paneer and peppers to the yoghurt marinade and leave for 1 hour to soak up the flavours. As it marinates, the paneer takes on a deeper colour from the saffron.

Preheat the grill (broiler) to a medium heat. Line a baking tray with foil or parchment paper and brush with a little of the saffron butter.

Thread the paneer and peppers onto the soaked wooden skewers and place on the tray. Cook the skewers under the grill for 3–4 minutes until the paneer softens and begins to turn light brown. Turn the skewers, baste with the saffron butter and grill for a further 4 minutes.

Remove the paneer and peppers from the skewers, transfer to a plate and sprinkle over the lime juice and chaat masala before serving with the mint raita.

# Paneer Skewers Stuffed with Mint & Coriander Chutney

## BHARWA PUDINA PANEER TIKKA

Paneer is a widely used cheese in Indian cooking and it's the perfect vehicle to absorb the flavours of herbs, spices and marinades. Sandwiching the mint and coriander (cilantro) stuffing between two pieces of paneer, before cooking the paneer under a hot grill until it softens with lightly charred edges, ensures there is loads of flavour.

500 g (1 lb 2 oz) paneer
melted butter, for basting
chaat masala, to garnish

### For the stuffing

80 g (2¾ oz) mint leaves
20 g (¾ oz) coriander (cilantro)
  leaves and stems
juice of 2 limes
pinch of salt

### For the marinade

5 tbsp Greek yoghurt
2 tsp chickpea (gram) flour
2 garlic cloves, roughly chopped
2 cm (½ in) ginger root,
  roughly chopped
2 green bird's-eye chillies
salt, to taste

Trim the edges from all sides of the block of paneer to neaten. Set aside the trimmings to add to the stuffing mixture. Cut the paneer into 4 equal pieces, then halve them lengthwise. Set aside while you make the stuffing and marinade.

To make the stuffing, put all the ingredients in a blender and blend to a smooth paste. (I find a NutriBullet works well for this.) The paste needs to be thick enough to stuff the paneer and so, only if absolutely necessary, add 1 tablespoon of water. Crush or grate (shred) the paneer trimmings, add them to the stuffing and mix well.

Spread 1 teaspoon of the mint stuffing between two layers of the paneer to make a little sandwich and set aside. Leave the remaining stuffing in the blender but add the Greek yoghurt, chickpea (gram) flour, garlic, ginger and green chillies and season to taste. Blend to a smooth marinade and then transfer to a large bowl.

Heat the grill (broiler) to a high heat. Line a baking tray with foil and place a wire rack over the tray.

Submerge the paneer sandwiches in the yoghurt marinade until well coated and then place on the wire rack. (If the sandwiches come apart and the filling does not stay in place, secure them with wooden skewers or toothpicks.)

Grill on a high heat for 6 minutes. Turn the paneer sandwiches over, baste with melted butter and grill for a further 6 minutes until charred around the edges and cooked all the way through. Finish with a pinch of chaat masala.

Serve warm with salad and chutney of your choice.

# BREADS

Freshly made naans, fluffy rotis and buttery kulchas are the backbone of Indian cuisine. The variety of breads in India is phenomenal and in this chapter I hope to showcase the different types that work well with tandoori meals and how to replicate their textures and flavours at home. Homemade breads should be soft and slightly stretchy with charred edges, like the Khamiri Roti (page 116). Making bread is a skill: it has taken me years to perfect the techniques, but don't let that put you off. I have developed my recipes to be foolproof, so more than anything they will give you the confidence to cook them often. To celebrate the multitude of Indian breads, I have included a streetfood favourite, the Keema Baida Roti (page 118), which is a stuffed layered bread. Served warm, these breads epitomize the pleasure of eating tandoori food. The key is to allow the bread to soak up the juices from the grilled tikkas and kebabs while acting as a vehicle for the tangy chutneys, refreshing salads and spice mixes, bringing the real taste of India to your dining table.

# Garlic & Ghee Naan

In our quest to achieve that classic tandoori flavour at home, we have celebrated and loved the naan for decades. It's no surprise that I have given into the obsession of mastering the art of a homemade naan! This frying-pan (skillet) version ticks all the boxes — pillowy, fluffy, charred around the edges and doused in garlicky ghee. Just the vehicle to mop up all the delicious goodness of a multitude of tandoori dishes.

1 tsp active dried yeast
1 tsp caster (superfine) sugar
30 ml (2 tbsp) warm water
240 g (8½ oz/2 cups) plain (all-purpose) flour, plus an extra 150 g (5¼ oz/1 cup) for kneading and rolling
1 tsp baking powder
salt, to taste
90 ml (3 fl oz/⅓ cup) whole (full-fat) milk
100 g (3½ oz) Greek yoghurt
4 tbsp melted ghee
3 garlic cloves, finely chopped
handful of finely chopped coriander (cilantro)

In a small bowl, combine the yeast and sugar, then mix in the warm water. Leave to rest for 10 minutes.

In a large mixing bowl, mix together the flour, baking powder and salt. Add the milk and yoghurt along with the yeast mixture to the dry ingredients and mix well to form a sticky dough. Cover the bowl with cling film (plastic wrap) and leave in a warm place for 1 hour. (I normally leave the bowl next to the Aga.)

Meanwhile, warm 3 tablespoons of the ghee in a saucepan over a low heat. (Set aside the remaining ghee for cooking the naan.) Add the garlic and fry for 30 seconds, then as soon as it changes colour slightly, take the pan off the heat and set aside so the garlic can infuse the ghee while you cook the naan.

Using around 70–80 g (2½–2¾ oz) of the extra flour, knead the dough for 3–4 minutes, making sure it is smooth as it becomes less sticky.

Divide the dough into 4 equal portions. Dusting with a little bit more of the remaining extra flour, roll out each portion to an 18 cm (7 in) round. The naan does not need to be perfectly round, it just needs to fit in your frying pan (skillet). Shape all four naans and brush the tops with some of the remaining ghee.

Heat a large, dry frying pan over a medium-high heat.

As the pan begins to heat up, slap the ghee-coated side of a naan onto the hot pan. Cover with a lid and cook for 1 minute while bubbles begin to form on the surface. Do not lift the lid before 1 minute for the first naan, although you may need less time for this stage as you cook more breads and the pan gets hotter. Brush the top side with more of the melted ghee, then carefully flip the naan over and cook for a further 1½ minutes to brown on the other side. Wrap the naan in foil to keep warm while you cook the remaining breads.

While the naans are warm, pour over the garlicky ghee, top with the chopped coriander (cilantro) and serve with your favourite snacks or grilled food.

Garlic & Ghee Naan

BREADS

# Gram Flour Flatbread with Turmeric, Coriander & Carom Seeds

## PUNJABI MISSI ROTI

A delicious rustic flatbread made with chickpea or gram flour that's so simple to cook. The dough is mixed with onion, turmeric, coriander (cilantro), carom seeds and yoghurt. In India, adding yoghurt to breads is a common practice as it helps to keep the bread soft after it has been cooked.

200 g (7 oz/1¼ cups) chapatti flour (*atta*)

50 g (1¾ oz/scant ½ cup) chickpea (gram) flour

40 g (1½ oz) white onion, finely chopped

2 tbsp dried fenugreek leaves (*kasoori methi*) or you can add any fresh greens, if you prefer

1 tbsp chopped coriander (cilantro) leaves

1 heaped tsp carom seeds (*ajwain*)

1 tsp ground turmeric

1 tbsp Greek yoghurt

2 tsp melted ghee, plus extra for frying

salt, to taste

Combine both the flours in a large mixing bowl with the onion, fenugreek leaves, coriander (cilantro), carom seeds, turmeric and salt. Add the yoghurt and ghee, then mix in 150 ml (5½ fl oz/scant ⅔ cup) of water, a little at a time, to make a firm, stiff dough. Knead the dough either in the bowl or on a clean work surface for 2–3 minutes. Cover the bowl with cling film (plastic wrap) and leave the dough to rest for 30 minutes.

Divide the dough into 8 equal portions. Heat a dry frying pan (skillet) over a medium heat.

Working with one portion at a time, roll out the dough on a lightly floured work surface to a 20 cm (8 in) round.

Add ½ teaspoon of the ghee to the pan and then add the roti. Cover the pan with foil or a lid and cook for 2 minutes. Smear some more ghee on the top of the roti, flip it over and cook for a further 2 minutes on the other side. Spread more ghee over the top of the roti and then wrap it in foil or parchment paper to keep it warm while you cook the remaining breads.

Serve warm with yoghurt or pickle.

# Quick Tawa Roti

This has been my go-to recipe for years and definitely the one I turn to when I'm rushed for time. Every grilled meat or vegetable kebab needs a perfect soft flatbread as a base and this one ticks all the boxes. You can cook this on a barbeque or even in a griddle pan. I use a dry frying pan (skillet) and then finish it over an open flame for a wonderful charred flavour.

220 g (7¾ oz/1¾ cups) very strong white bread flour
40 ml (1¼ fl oz/2¾ tbsp) vegetable oil
pinch of salt

Combine the flour, oil and salt in a large mixing bowl. Gradually add 100 ml (3½ fl oz/scant ½ cup) of water and knead to a soft dough. Cover the bowl with cling film (plastic wrap) and leave to rest for 30 minutes.

Heat a large, dry frying pan (skillet) over a medium heat.

Knead the dough again on a lightly floured work surface. Divide the dough into 5 equal portions. Working with one portion at a time, roll out the dough to a 15 cm (6 in) round.

Add the roti to the pan and cook for 30 seconds on each side as bubbles form. Using tongs to hold the roti, cook the bread directly over a gas flame for 3 seconds on each side until lightly charred.

Serve warm with tikkas, chutneys and salads.

# Spiced Flatbread with Kashmiri Chilli & Carom Seeds

## KHAMIRI ROTI

This roti is a leavened bread that is very popular across the northern frontier and Delhi. Back in the day, the dough was left overnight to ferment. Nowadays, one way to help with the fermentation process is to use buttermilk, which gives the dough a slightly sour flavour. I have opted for a quicker version using dried yeast. Traditionally cooked in a tandoor, the trick to replicating the tandoori taste is cooking the roti over an open flame. A technique commonly used to cook Indian breads, always use a gas hob rather than induction.

2 tsp dried active yeast
1 tsp sugar
120 ml (4 fl oz/½ cup) warm whole (full-fat) milk
250 g (8¾ oz/1½ cups) chapatti flour (*atta*)
½ tsp carom seeds (*ajwain*)
¼ tsp Kashmiri chilli powder
pinch of salt
melted ghee, to finish

In a small bowl, combine the yeast and sugar, then mix in the warm milk. Stir well and set aside to rest for 10 minutes.

In a large mixing bowl, combine the flour, carom seeds, chilli powder and salt. Now, add the yeast mixture to the dry ingredients and stir well. Gradually add 4 tablespoons of water and knead to a soft dough. Cover the bowl with cling film (plastic wrap) and leave to rest for 1½ hours.

Heat a large, dry frying pan (skillet) over a high gas flame.

Divide the dough into 6 equal portions. Keep a bowl of water nearby. Working with one portion at a time, roll out the dough on a lightly floured work surface to an 18 cm (7 in) round.

Brush the roti evenly with water all over and then place in the hot pan. The water will make the roti stick to the pan. Flip the pan over so it is upside down and cook the roti directly over the open flame for 1 minute. This will give the bread a lovely tandoori flavour. Keep moving the pan over the flame so the roti browns evenly. Now turn the pan back over and place on the heat for 1 minute to cook through the base. Spread the roti with ghee and wrap in foil to keep warm while you cook the remaining breads.

# Crispy Fried Flatbread Stuffed with Spicy Lamb, Chilli & Coriander

## KEEMA BAIDA ROTI

Eating these stuffed roti at Bade Miyans in Mumbai as a teenager has always been one of my favourite food memories. The Mughlai community made this stuffed bread so popular that it's now a staple of streetfood stalls across India. Commonly served during festivities, a lot of places serve baida roti all year. Spicy ground lamb stuffed inside an eggy roti and fried in ghee, it's one of the highlights on Ramzan menus as well.

### For the filling

3 tbsp vegetable oil
5 green cardamom pods
100 g (3½ oz) onion, finely chopped
6 garlic cloves, ground to a paste
5 cm (2 in) ginger root, ground to a paste
2 tbsp tomato purée (paste)
350 g (12¼ oz) minced (ground) leg of lamb
1 tsp Kashmiri chilli powder (or mild unsmoked paprika)
2 tbsp dried fenugreek leaves (*kasoori methi*)
salt, to taste
1 tsp garam masala
1 green bird's-eye chilli, finely chopped
1 tbsp chopped coriander (cilantro) leaves
juice of ½ lime

### For the baida roti

210 g (7½ oz/1½ cups) plain (all-purpose) flour
1 tbsp vegetable oil
pinch of sea salt
2–3 eggs
50 g (2 oz) ghee, for rolling and frying

To make the filling, heat the oil in a non-stick saucepan over a medium heat. Add the cardamom pods and fry for 10 seconds. Add the onion and fry for 7–8 minutes until light brown. Add the garlic and ginger pastes and cook, stirring frequently, for 1 minute. Stir in the tomato purée (paste) and fry for 2 minutes.

Add the minced (ground) lamb and cook, stirring continuously, for 3 minutes. Add the chilli powder, stir well and cook for 2 minutes until the meat is evenly coloured all the way through. Add the fenugreek leaves, season to taste, cover with a lid and simmer over a low heat for 4 minutes until everything is mixed well. Turn off the heat and add the garam masala, green chilli, chopped coriander (cilantro) and lime juice. Tilt the saucepan slightly and spoon off any excess oil. Leave the keema to cool completely before making the baida roti.

To make the roti, combine the flour, oil and salt in a large mixing bowl. Mix well, then gradually add 110 ml (3¾ fl oz/½ cup) of water, a little at a time. Knead as the dough begins to come together. Leave the dough in the bowl, cover with cling film (plastic wrap) and set aside to rest for 1 hour.

Divide both the dough and filling mixture into 4 equal portions. Break one egg into a bowl, whisk lightly and set aside.

Heat a non-stick frying pan (skillet) over a medium heat.

Working with one portion at a time, add a little ghee to the dough and roll out as thinly as possible to a 25 cm (10 in) round. The roti does not need to be perfectly round — that is not essential for a baida roti.

Spoon one portion of the filling mixture into the middle of the roti, make a little well in the keema and add half of the beaten egg. Working quickly, fold the sides of the roti inwards overlapping one another to form a neat parcel.

Add 1 teaspoon of the ghee to the pan. Carefully lift the baida roti parcel, place it in the pan and fry over a medium heat for 3–4 minutes on one side. Top the roti with a little ghee, flip it over and cook for 3–4 minutes on the other side. Press down lightly on the parcel to ensure the filling is cooked through. Flip the roti over again and cook for a further 2 minutes. Keep warm while you make and cook the remaining baida roti.

Serve warm with lime wedges, chutney and salad.

# Mint Paratha with Chilli, Cumin & Chaat Masala

PUDINE KA PARATHA

Mint is used widely in dishes across India from curries, chutneys, salads and even in breads. Here I have used the base recipe of my lachha paratha and added fresh mint to the dough. The word 'lachha' means layers and this paratha is flaky buttery and delicious. Adding the spice mix between layers brings so much more flavour to the bread as it cooks. If you simply prefer a plain lachha paratha, you can still make the very same recipe and omit the fresh mint and spice mix.

210 g (7½ oz/1½ cups) plain (all-purpose) flour, plus extra for dusting
1 tbsp vegetable oil
pinch of sea salt
20 g (¾ oz) fresh mint leaves, finely chopped
melted ghee, for brushing and frying

### For the spice mix

2 tsp dried mint leaves
½ tsp cumin seeds, coarsely crushed
1 tsp Kashmiri chilli powder
2 tsp chaat masala

Combine the flour, oil and salt in a large mixing bowl. Add the mint, mix well and then gradually add 110 ml (3¾ fl oz/½ cup) of water, a little at a time, and knead as the dough begins to come together. Cover the bowl with cling film (plastic wrap) and leave the dough to rest for 1 hour.

Mix together all the spice mix ingredients in a small bowl and set aside.

Divide the dough into 5 equal portions. Working with one portion at a time, roll out the dough as thinly as possible. Brush with a thin layer of ghee and sprinkle with a generous pinch of the spice mix.

Starting at the end closest to you, roll the paratha away from you to form a long snake. Now coil one end of the snake inwards until it meets the other end. Flatten slightly and set aside. Repeat with the remaining dough, cover and leave to rest again for 1 hour.

Heat a large, dry frying pan (skillet) over a medium heat.

Working with one coil at a time, roll out the dough to a 20 cm (8 in) round, dusting with a little extra flour to make sure it does not stick.

Add the paratha to the pan and cook for 1 minute on each side. Add 1 teaspoon of ghee to the pan, flip over the paratha and fry for 1 minute until it goes light brown and flaky. Smear the top side with a little more ghee and flip over again. Cook for a further 1 minute, drizzling with a little more ghee, until it has turned light brown and is cooked all the way through. Wrap the paratha in foil or a clean cloth to keep warm while you cook the remaining breads.

Serve warm with the curry of your choice or some chutneys and pickle.

# Millet Flatbread with Chilli, Fenugreek, Carom Seeds & Sesame Seeds

## BAJRA METHI PARATHA

I have been wanting to share a recipe using pearl millet flour, also known as bajra, for such a long time. It's a nutritious variety of flour that is widely grown across India and so it's nice to see many more places in the UK now stocking bajra. As it's a gluten-free flour, you need the addition of chapatti flour to help bind everything together while making the dough. This paratha is flavoured with green chilli, fresh fenugreek leaves, carom seeds and sesame seeds to aid digestion and packed the bread with flavour.

80 g (2¾ oz/⅓ cup) pearl millet flour (*bajra*)
80 g (2¾ oz/⅓ cup) chapatti flour (*atta*), plus extra for dusting
1 tbsp vegetable oil
1 tbsp Greek yoghurt
1 green bird's-eye chilli, finely chopped
50 g (1¾ oz) fresh fenugreek leaves (*methi*)
1 tsp carom seeds (*ajwain*)
1 heaped tsp sesame seeds
1 tsp ground turmeric
salt, to taste
60 ml (4 tbsp) water
melted butter or ghee, for frying

Combine all the ingredients, except the water, in a large mixing bowl and stir well. Now add 1 tablespoon of the water and knead as the flour comes together. Add more of the water, a little at a time, until the dough forms. It might seem grainy at first, but as you continue to knead, the dough will get smoother. Cover the bowl and set aside to rest for 10 minutes.

Divide the dough into 5 equal portions. Heat a dry frying pan (skillet) over a medium heat.

Working with one portion at a time, roll out the dough on a lightly floured work surface to an 18 cm (7 in) round.

Add the paratha to the hot pan and cook for 1 minute on one side. Flip over the paratha, spread ghee across the top and cook on the other side for 1 minute. Flip again, spread a little more ghee over the top and cook for a further 1 minute. Flip again and cook for 20 seconds. Wrap the paratha in a clean cloth or parchment paper to keep warm while you cook the remaining breads.

Serve with chutney or pickle.

# Saffron–Infused Milk Bread with Cardamom & Rose Water

## SHEERMAL

One of my first food festivals nearly 15 years ago was at the Southbank Centre in London. It felt like a good opportunity to introduce sheermal to the local audience who had never tasted this bread before. A saffron-infused milk bread flavoured with cardamom and rose water, sheermal is such a classic recipe from the north of India and works brilliantly with tandoori dishes and stir fries as well as chutneys. Baking the bread in the oven turns the edges slightly brown, which has hints of savoury and sweet, as well as subtle floral notes from the rose water, which balances everything.

pinch of saffron strands
170 ml (5¾ fl oz/¾ cup) hot whole (full-fat) milk
1 tsp fast action yeast
280 g (10 oz/2¼ cups) plain (all-purpose) flour
½ tsp ground cardamom
3 tsp sugar
pinch of salt
1 tsp rose water
1 tbsp melted butter or ghee

Put the saffron in a bowl and add 2 tablespoons of the hot milk. Set aside to let the flavours infuse until the breads are ready to cook.

Put the yeast in a separate small bowl and add the remaining hot milk and leave to dissolve for 3–4 minutes.

In a large mixing bowl, combine the flour, cardamom, sugar and salt. Add the rose water and butter or ghee. Now, gradually add the yeast mixture, mixing everything together to form a slightly sticky dough. Cover the bowl with cling film (plastic wrap) and set aside to rest in a warm place for 30 minutes.

Preheat the oven to 210°C fan (450°F/gas 8). Line two large baking trays with parchment paper.

Divide the dough into 4 equal portions. Working with one portion at a time, roll out the dough on a lightly floured work surface to an 18 cm (7 in) round. Repeat with a second portion of dough and transfer both rounds to one of the baking trays, if your baking tray can fit two sheermals.

Place the tray in the oven and cook for 4–5 minutes. Remove the tray from the oven and brush the breads with the saffron-infused milk. Return the tray to the oven to cook for a further 5 minutes until light brown but also bright yellow from the saffron. Remove the sheermal from the oven, wrap in foil or a clean cloth while you cook the remaining breads.

Serve with tikkas and kebabs.

# Flatbread Stuffed with Grated Paneer, Green Chilli, Ginger & Mint

## PANEER KULCHA

Awadhi cooking is synonymous with ostentatious food. Their recipes are a true celebration. Kulcha is a lightly leavened flatbread enjoyed in homes and restaurants primarily across the regions of Punjab, Uttar Pradesh and Uttarakhand. I have adapted the traditional recipe to be cooked on a stove top and yet still give you a taste of the tandoor as the bread cooks in butter until crispy around the edges. Kulcha can be made without any stuffing although the addition of grated (shredded) paneer with spices and herbs is truly special. Serve as an accompaniment to tikkas and salad or simply eat this just with some chutney.

### For the dough

210 g (7½ oz/1½ cups) plain
  (all-purpose) flour
pinch of salt
pinch of sugar
1 tsp baking powder
1 tbsp vegetable oil
2 tbsp Greek yoghurt
90–100 ml (3–3½ fl oz/⅓–scant
  ½ cup) whole (full-fat) milk
melted butter, for frying
handful of finely chopped
  coriander (cilantro)

### For the stuffing

200 g (7 oz) paneer, finely grated
  (shredded)
5 cm (2 in) ginger root,
  finely chopped
2 green bird's-eye chillies,
  finely chopped
10 g (⅓ oz) fresh mint leaves,
  finely chopped
2 tsp chaat masala
1 tsp cumin seeds,
  coarsely crushed
½ tsp Kashmiri chilli powder

Combine all the dough ingredients, except the butter and chopped coriander (cilantro), in a large mixing bowl. Mix well and knead to a dough. Cover the bowl with cling film (plastic wrap) and set aside for to rest 45 minutes.

In a separate large mixing bowl, mix together all the stuffing ingredients and knead lightly. Divide into 5 equal portions, roll each one into a ball and set aside.

Heat a large, dry frying pan (skillet) over a medium heat.

Divide the dough into 5 equal portions. Working with one portion at a time, roll out the dough to a 10 cm (4 in) round. Place one ball of stuffing in the middle of the round and then pull the edges of the dough up and over to cover the stuffing. Dip in a little flour and roll out on a work surface to an 18 cm (7 in) round.

Place the paneer kulcha in the hot pan and cook for 2 minutes. Spread some butter over the top of the kulcha, flip it over and cook for a further 2 minutes. Top with more butter, flip again and cook for a further 2 minutes until it turns light brown. Wrap the kulcha in foil or parchment paper to keep warm while you cook the remaining breads.

Serve with tikkas and salad or simply with a chutney.

# CONDIMENTS

Fresh chutneys, dips and other sauces bring everything from fiery heat, smoky notes, sharp acidity, touches of sweetness and contrasting textures to your tandoori feast. There is a variety to choose from in this chapter: freshly made chutneys that are quick to rustle up sit alongside slow-cooked chutneys with a longer shelf life once jarred and refrigerated. All these recipes are such a vital part of snacking the Indian way. Heat comes from chillies that are fresh, dried or pounded into a powder, all lending varied flavour profiles. Smokiness is from the vegetables that are charred over an open flame or the addition of a smoked butter, which amplifies the tandoori taste in every dish. Acidity is provided by sour lemons, limes, mangoes, vinegar and tamarind — ingredients that cut through the richness of the meat, chicken and vegetables in this book — adding freshness and zing. My Seb aur Adrak ki Chutney (page 130) and Aam Chundo (page 131) are just two of the hero recipes to make when you have some time to prepare them in advance. Thinking seasonally, making chutneys is also the perfect way to preserve fruits and vegetables.

CONDIMENTS

# Roasted Tomato Chutney

## BHUNE TAMATAR KI CHUTNEY

Living in India, it was a weekly ritual to have friends round to our home on Sundays, when late afternoon was a time for drinks, snacks and chutneys. This roasted tomato chutney was always on our table, served alongside crispy fried pakoras or paneer tikkas. It's similar to Bihari Chokha, roasted mashed vegetables cooked with spices, which is served as an accompaniment with traditional breads. This fiery chutney is spiked with garlic, chilli and coriander (cilantro) for bursts of flavour, while the charred tomatoes lend a roasted, smoky flavour to the chutney. After roasting, you can finish the tomatoes either under a hot grill (broiler) or over an open flame. Tamatar ki Chutney is perfect for spooning over tikkas and for topping freshly made flatbreads.

680 g (1 lb 8 oz) tomatoes,
  halved
3 tbsp mustard oil
1 tsp sugar
6 garlic cloves, finely chopped
½ tsp Kashmiri chilli powder
2 tbsp finely chopped coriander
  (cilantro) leaves
salt, to taste

Preheat the oven to 220°C fan (475°F/gas 9). Line a baking tray with parchment paper or foil and set a wire rack over the tray.

In a bowl, mix the tomatoes with 1 tablespoon of the mustard oil, sugar and a pinch of salt. Lay the tomatoes cut side down on the wire rack, place the tray in the hot oven and roast for 20 minutes until softened.

Preheat the grill (broiler) to a high heat. Put the tray of roasted tomatoes under the hot grill on the top shelf and grill for 10 minutes or until charred and slightly blackened. Set aside to cool.

Using a blender, blitz half of the tomatoes until smooth and pour into a serving bowl. Roughly chop the remaining tomatoes and add them to the bowl.

Heat the remaining mustard oil in a frying pan (skillet) over a medium heat. Add the garlic and fry for a 1 minute. Turn off the heat and stir in the chilli powder, then pour this mixture over the tomato chutney. Garnish with the chopped coriander (cilantro) and season to taste.

This chutney will keep for up to 3–4 days when stored in the fridge.

# Apple & Ginger Chutney

**SEB AUR ADRAK KI CHUTNEY**

A sweet and spicy chutney that is just as great served at a barbeque as it is eaten alongside curries. The apples are simmered slowly with fennel, cardamom and chilli to a rich, sticky consistency. As it cooks, the chutney turns a lovely dark colour. Heading into the cooler months, I find this is the best way to use up the abundance of apples from my garden. A homemade chutney makes the perfect food gift.

2 tbsp vegetable oil

2 tsp fennel seeds, coarsely crushed in a pestle and mortar

60 g (2 oz) white onion, thinly sliced

800 g (1 lb 12 oz) cooking apples, peeled, cored and diced

3 tsp grated (shredded) ginger root

1 tsp Kashmiri chilli powder (or mild chilli powder)

180 g (6¼ oz/1 scant cup) dark soft brown sugar

4 tbsp white wine vinegar

pinch of salt

Heat the oil in a heavy-based saucepan on a medium heat. Add the coarsely crushed fennel seeds and let them sizzle for 1 minute. Add the sliced onion and fry for 5–7 minutes until they begin to soften and change colour.

At this stage add the diced apple, grated (shredded) ginger, chilli powder, sugar, vinegar and salt. Stir thoroughly, making sure all the apple pieces are coated in the spices. Reduce the heat to low, cover with a lid and gently simmer for 1 hour, stirring halfway through. The chutney will thicken, caramelize and turn syrupy. Leave to cool completely.

Once cool, transfer the chutney to sterilized jars, seal and store in the fridge. Once opened, keep refrigerated and use within 2 weeks.

# Mango & Chilli Chutney

## AAM CHUNDO

SERVES 4–6 AS AN
ACCOMPANIMENT

The mango season in India has always been very short, so living in Britain, over time I have adapted this family recipe to use up mangoes that are widely available in supermarkets. The key is to get the unripe green variety which holds its shape while you grate it. Infused with cumin and chilli, this chutney is sticky, sweet and spicy and makes the perfect condiment for a tandoori feast or even served as a late-night snack simply with paratha. This chutney has a longer shelf life than most others in this chapter.

2 tbsp vegetable oil

1 tbsp cumin seeds,
    coarsely crushed

700 g (1 lb 8½ oz) green mango,
    peeled and coarsely grated
    (shredded)

500 g (1 lb 2 oz/2½ cups) caster
    (superfine) sugar

3 tsp Kashmiri chilli powder

pinch of salt

Heat the oil in a large saucepan over a low heat. Add the cumin seeds and then, as they begin to sizzle, tip in the grated (shredded) mango. Stir well.

Turn up the heat to medium. Add the sugar and, stirring continuously, cook for 10 minutes until the sugar has dissolved. At this point, the chutney will still have a lot of liquid; this is fine as the chutney will thicken as it cools.

Turn off the heat and stir in the chilli powder and salt. Continue stirring for 5 minutes to make sure the sugar does not crystallize as the chutney cools. Cover and leave to cool completely.

Once cool, transfer the chutney to a sterilized jar, seal and store in the fridge. This chundo can be eaten straightaway, but once opened, keep refrigerated, and use within 2 weeks.

# Sweet & Spicy Lemon Pickle

## LIMBACHI CHATNI

A sweet and spicy lemon pickle that is perfect to serve with everything. And I do mean absolutely everything. While sipping chai, my mother would prepare the lemons, mixing the citrus fruit with spices and salt, and then decant everything into large storage jars, known as barnis. These jars were left in the sun so the lemons would pickle and soften. The sun's hot rays peeking through — and knowing that this heat was creating so much goodness inside our pickle jars — was a sight I always loved. It's a lengthy process, but one that is well worth the time. If, like me, you live in a country where the days are short and the nights are cold, this gem of a recipe is a quicker version of the classic lemon pickle from my hometown in Maharashtra. It's just what you need for a sweet, sour, spicy and tart condiment.

You will need 1 x 350 ml (12 fl oz) jar, sterilized

3 unwaxed lemons
2 tsp sea salt
80 g (2¾ oz/⅓ cup) caster (superfine) sugar
1 heaped tsp Kashmiri chilli powder
½ tsp cumin seeds, coarsely crushed

Cut the lemons into quarters and slice each wedge into three pieces. Remove any pips and then put the lemon pieces in a non-reactive saucepan with 200 ml (6¾ fl oz/¾ cup) of water and the salt. Cook over a medium heat for 17–18 minutes until the lemon rind softens and turns a lighter yellow colour. Leave to cool slightly and then drain the cooking water into a separate bowl. (This lemon cooking water can be used for curries or stews).

Transfer the cooked lemons to a mixing bowl. Add the sugar, chilli powder and cumin seeds. Stir thoroughly until the sugar has dissolved.

Spoon the lemons into a sterilized jar, seal and leave to pickle overnight. When refrigerated, this chutney will keep for up to 2 weeks.

# Spicy Coconut & Cashew Chutney

## NARIYAL AUR KAJU KI CHUTNEY

So many streetfood snacks across India include this popular chutney; creamy fresh coconut tempered with smoky dried red chilli, curry leaves and flavoured with tangy tamarind paste. This fresh chutney is so versatile that it's great to add even to sandwiches. I have blended the coconut with cashew nuts to give the chutney an even richer, creamier consistency and I use frozen, grated (shredded) coconut that further thickens the chutney once it has defrosted.

50 g (1¾ oz/⅔ cup) grated (shredded) coconut (I use frozen, but you can use fresh)
30 g (1 oz/¼ cup) roasted cashew nuts
1 tbsp roasted chana dal
2 green bird's-eye chillies
1 tsp tamarind paste
1 tsp caster (superfine) sugar
salt, to taste

### For the tempering

2 tbsp vegetable oil
1 dried mild red chilli
10–12 curry leaves
1 tsp black mustard seeds
pinch of asafoetida

Put the grated (shredded) coconut, cashew nuts, chana dal, green chillies, tamarind paste and sugar in a blender with 100 ml (3½ fl oz/scant ½ cup) of water. Blend to a smooth, fine paste. Check the seasoning and add salt to taste, then transfer to a serving dish.

To make the tempering, heat the oil in a small frying pan (skillet) over a medium heat. Add the mustard seeds, dried chilli, asafoetida and curry leaves, stir for a few seconds and then take the pan off the heat. Pour this flavoured oil over the chutney in the dish and serve immediately.

*See photos on pages 134–5.*

Spicy Coconut & Cashew Chutney

# Spicy Green Chilli Chutney

## HARI MIRCH KI CHUTNEY

SERVES 4 AS AN
ACCOMPANIMENT

Green chillies can be an underrated ingredient when it comes to adding a blast of heat to meals. It's common for Indians to have a green bird's-eye chilli on their plate to enjoy as they eat. This dip celebrates the fiery bird's-eye chilli and is packed with added flavour from fresh coriander (cilantro) and lime. But what is the secret ingredient? A green apple that lends depth and a sour note to the chutney. Think Indian tomatillo that's zingy, hot and spicy and works well on tandoori paneer, grilled meats, salads and stuffed inside flatbreads.

7 green bird's-eye chillies (reduce to 5 if you prefer less heat)
30 g (1 oz) coriander (cilantro) leaves, roughly chopped
150 g (5¼ oz) Granny Smith apple, roughly chopped
1 garlic clove
salt, to taste
4 tsp caster (superfine) sugar
juice of 2 limes
1 tsp crushed cumin seeds

Place all the ingredients in a blender and blitz to a smooth paste. Do not add any water. Serve with rotis, kebabs and salads.

The chutney will keep for up to 2–3 days when stored in a non-reactive bowl in the fridge.

# Sesame & Chilli Chutney

## TIL KI CHUTNEY

SERVES 4 AS AN
ACCOMPANIMENT

Hailing from the northern region of Uttarakhand, Til ki Chutney is a spicy dipping sauce that is commonly eaten with parathas or grilled snacks. For this chutney, white sesame seeds are lightly toasted and then blended with fresh mint leaves, green chillies and tamarind paste.

3 tbsp white sesame seeds
10 g (⅓ oz) fresh mint leaves
1 green bird's-eye chilli
1 tbsp tamarind paste
2 tsp caster (superfine) sugar
salt, to taste

Heat a small, dry frying pan (skillet) over a medium heat. Add the sesame seeds to the pan and toast for 2 minutes, shaking the pan often, until they turn light brown. Set aside to cool.

Once cool, grind the toasted sesame seeds to a coarse powder in a blender and transfer to a serving bowl.

Using the same blender, blitz the mint leaves, green chilli, tamarind paste, sugar and salt to a paste with 50 ml (1¾ fl oz/ ¼ cup) of water. Add this paste to the sesame seeds in the bowl, mix well and serve immediately.

# Tangy Tamarind Chutney

**IMLI KI CHUTNEY**

SERVES 4 AS AN
ACCOMPANIMENT

Walking through the by-lanes of Old Delhi, you will find the streetfood institution Parathewalli Galli. 'Galli' means street and this street is renowned for parathas of every variety. One of the condiments served alongside the stuffed breads is their signature Imli ki Chutney. The tangy tamarind works really well as a dip for parathas and other snacks. To my surprise, the chutney includes crushed banana, which lends a wonderful sweetness as well as a thick consistency to the chutney. As always with tamarind paste, the strength and colour can vary, so tailor the quantity used according to the quality of your paste.

2 tbsp raisins
150 ml (5½ fl oz/scant ⅔ cup) warm water
150 g (5¼ oz) banana
4 tbsp tamarind paste (check the strength and adjust to taste)
6 tbsp jaggery or dark soft brown sugar
¼ tsp cumin seeds
½ tsp Kashmiri chilli powder
¼ tsp black salt

Place the raisins in a bowl with 100 ml (3½ fl oz/scant ½ cup) of the warm water. Set aside to soak for 10 minutes.

Peel and chop the banana. Blend the raisins with their soaking liquid in a blender along with half the chopped banana, the tamarind paste, jaggery or sugar, cumin seeds, chilli powder and black salt.

Add the remaining 50 ml (1½ fl oz/¼ cup) of warm water to thin the chutney. Serve immediately in a bowl topped with the remaining banana to accompany kebabs, cutlets and rotis.

# Mustard Chutney

**SARSON KI CHUTNEY**

SERVES 4 AS AN
ACCOMPANIMENT

A classic dish that is commonly made across the north and east of India. This recipe uses black mustard seeds that are coarsely crushed with garlic, green chilli and turmeric to create a chutney with the required pungency to pair with kebabs and flatbreads.

6 tbsp black mustard seeds
4 tbsp Greek yoghurt
4 garlic cloves
4 green bird's-eye chillies
3 tsp caster (superfine) sugar
salt, to taste
1 tbsp vegetable oil
½ tsp ground turmeric

Add the mustard seeds to a blender and grind to a coarse powder. Transfer to a serving bowl.

In the same blender, combine 2 tablespoons of the yoghurt with the garlic, chillies, sugar and salt. Blend to a smooth paste. Transfer this paste to the bowl with the ground mustard seeds and add the remaining yoghurt. Mix well.

Heat the oil in a frying pan (skillet) over a medium heat. Add the turmeric and fry for a few seconds. Pour this flavoured oil over the mustard chutney, stir well and serve immediately.

# Coconut & Cucumber Yoghurt with Chilli, Mustard Seeds & Curry Leaves

## CUCUMBER PACHADI

A cooling coconut and cucumber yoghurt raita from the Telangana region, which is mixed with a tempering of smoky dried chillies, mustard seeds, turmeric and curry leaves. It's the tempering on this pachadi that really makes it for me. Serve chilled with roti, paratha or even just plain rice.

100 g (3½ oz) grated (shredded) frozen or fresh coconut
2 tsp black mustard seeds
1 tsp cumin seeds
1 green bird's-eye chilli
6 tbsp Greek yoghurt
450 g (1 lb) cucumber, coarsely grated (shredded) — do not drain the water from the cucumber
2 tsp caster (superfine) sugar
salt, to taste
chopped coriander (cilantro), to garnish

### For the tempering

2 tbsp vegetable or coconut oil
1 tsp black mustard seeds
2 dried mild red chillies
10–12 curry leaves
½ tsp ground turmeric

Put the grated (shredded) coconut in a blender along with the mustard seeds, cumin seeds, green chilli and the yoghurt. Blend to a smooth paste, then transfer to a serving bowl and stir in the grated (shredded) cucumber and sugar. Season well to balance the pungency of the mustard seeds and chilli.

For the tempering, heat the oil in a small frying pan (skillet) over a medium heat. Add the mustard seeds and, as they splutter, quickly add the dried chillies, curry leaves and turmeric. Turn off the heat, then pour this flavoured oil over the pachadi in the bowl and stir well. Garnish with coriander (cilantro) before serving.

This chutney can be made ahead of time — up to a day before serving — and stored in the fridge to allow the flavours of the tempering to infuse the cucumber yoghurt.

# Spiced Potato Raita with Cumin & Chilli

## ALOO CHANNE KA RAITA

A cooling raita with crushed potatoes and chickpeas, combined with a mix of coarse spices that lend texture, warmth and flavour. This is a classic condiment that is commonly served with streetfood.

100 g (3½ oz) canned chickpeas (garbanzo beans), drained
320 g (11¼ oz) plain yoghurt
1 heaped tsp ground coriander
½ tsp ground cumin
1 tsp dried mango powder
1 tsp Kashmiri chilli powder
2 tsp caster (superfine) sugar
salt, to taste
handful of chopped coriander (cilantro) leaves
300 g (10½ oz) potatoes, peeled, boiled and cooled

Place the chickpeas (garbanzo beans) in a small saucepan, cover with water and bring to a boil. Reduce the heat to medium and simmer the chickpeas for 20 minutes. Drain and set aside to cool slightly.

In a large mixing bowl, mix the yoghurt with 100 ml (3½ fl oz/scant ½ cup) of water and whisk until smooth. Stir in the spices, sugar, salt and coriander (cilantro).

Roughly crush the potatoes and add them to the bowl with the yoghurt mixture. Next, roughly crush the cooked chickpeas add these to the raita. Stir well and serve.

This raita can be made ahead of time and stored in the fridge until ready to serve.

# Mint Raita

## PUDINE KA RAITA

One of my favourite recipes for adding that required mint flavour to grilled food, kebabs and salads. This raita has layers and layers of flavour from all the spices included, while the mint makes it simultaneously cooling as well as spicy.

150 g (5¼ oz) Greek yoghurt
2 spring onions (scallions), roughly chopped
1 cm (½ in) ginger root, roughly chopped
30 g (1 oz) fresh mint leaves
10 g (⅓ oz) fresh coriander (cilantro) leaves and stems
1 tsp cumin seeds, roasted and coarsely ground
½ tsp black salt
pinch of sea salt

Place the yoghurt, spring onions (scallions), ginger, mint and coriander (cilantro) leaves and stems in a blender. Add 80 ml (2¾ fl oz/⅓ cup) of water and blend to a smooth paste. Pour into a serving bowl.

Combine the crushed cumin seeds, black salt and sea salt in a small bowl. Sprinkle this spice mix over the raita and chill in the fridge.

Serve chilled with your choice of kebab, snack or salad.

# Tangy Chilli & Coriander Dipping Sauce

## SIRKEWALLA MIRCH AUR DHANIA

There are many streetfood stalls and restaurants that serve a vinegar-based dipping sauce. One of my first encounters tasting this was when my local kathi roll stall in Bandra, Mumbai, added it to the roll. The base dipping sauce is fairly simple, but I wanted to dial up the flavour quotient so my version of this sauce packs a real punch. It's perfect over any grilled meats, veggies or even just to dip some bread in. Make it ahead of time as the longer the green chillies can soak, the more they pickle and soften in the vinegar.

100 ml (3½ fl oz/scant ½ cup) white wine vinegar
4 tbsp caster (superfine) sugar
pinch of salt
3 green bird's-eye chillies, finely chopped
2 tbsp finely chopped coriander (cilantro) leaves
1 tbsp finely chopped coriander (cilantro) stems

Mix the vinegar with the sugar, salt and 50 ml (1¾ fl oz/¼ cup) of water in a serving dish. Stir well until the sugar has dissolved completely.

Add the green chillies, chopped coriander (cilantro) leaves and stems to the vinegar mixture and set aside for 1 hour to allow the flavours to mellow slightly before serving.

This dipping sauce can be made a day ahead and stored in the fridge.

# Grilled Lemons

This has to be the flavour of my childhood. As a girl, I watched the street vendor dip charred lemons in chilli powder and then smear them over grilled corn-on-the-cobs. The freshness of lemon cuts through the grilled tandoori flavours and richness of marinade-smothered tikkas. Grilling lemons imparts a smokiness to the fruit and when squeezed over meat or fish gives everything a wonderful tang.

lemons, halved

Warm a griddle pan over a high heat. Place the lemon halves, cut side down, on the pan and griddle for 1–2 minutes. As the lemons begins to char, remove them from the pan.

Squeeze over your favourite kebabs, salads or chutneys for a tangy, smoky flavour.

# Spiced Pickled Red Onions

## SIRKEWALLA PYAZ

No Indian meal is complete without tangy pickled onions. This speedy recipe has them doused in lime juice and salt instead of vinegar and finished with ground spices and fresh coriander (cilantro).

300 g (10½ oz) red onion,
    thinly sliced
juice of 1 lemon
generous pinch of salt
½ tsp Kashmiri chilli powder
½ tsp coarsely crushed
    cumin seeds
1 tbsp finely chopped coriander
    (cilantro) leaves, to garnish

Put the onion in a large bowl along with the lemon juice and salt. Set aside for 2–3 hours to allow the onions to soften. (You can also leave the onions to pickle overnight in the fridge so they turn a deep purple colour.)

When ready to serve, top the onions with chilli powder, crushed cumin and chopped coriander (cilantro). Mix well and serve with kebabs and tikkas.

# Pickled Whole Chillies

## SIRKEWALLI MIRCH

The best part of the growing season is the glut of chillies that ripen on my windowsill every few weeks. They are all different colours and sizes so this pickled chilli recipe is perfect as they soak up the spiced vinegar dressing and taste wonderful with tikkas, kebabs or even as a side with curries. The spiced vinegar base from this recipe can also be used to pickle other vegetables, including carrots and cabbage, which are equally delicious served as a condiment.

You will need 1 x 750 ml (25 fl oz) jar, sterilized

12 mixed chillies, left whole if small or halved lengthwise if large
1 tsp black peppercorns
1 tsp yellow mustard seeds
2 dried bay leaves
500 ml (17 fl oz/2 cups) white wine vinegar
1 tsp caster (superfine) sugar
pinch of salt

Put the chillies, peppercorns, mustard seeds and bay leaves in the sterilized jar. Add the vinegar to the jar along with 250 ml (8½ fl oz/1 cup) of water, the sugar and a pinch of salt. Stir to mix, seal the jar and leave for 1 week to allow the chillies to pickle. Serve with kebabs or stuffed in naan or roti.

Once opened, the pickled chillies will keep for up to 2 weeks when stored in the fridge.

# Smoked Butter

One of the key elements of cooking in a tandoor or over coals is the wonderful smoky flavour that lingers even as you serve the food. One way to achieve this distinctive smoky aroma and taste is to adopt the dhungar method. I have used this method of smoking ingredients in my recipe for Aslam Butter Chicken on page 32 and on many other occasions for recipes in my cookbooks. With grilled and pan-fried dishes, the simplest way I have found to achieve that aromatic, warm and intense smokiness is to have large quantity of smoked butter on hand that can be used for basting.

You will need 1 x 250 g (8¾ oz) jar, sterilized

250 g (8¾ oz) butter
1 medium piece of coal

Melt the butter in a saucepan with a lid. Set aside.

Turn the gas hob to a high heat. Using tongs, place the piece of coal directly in the open flame. Turn it a few times as it begins to heat up and glow.

Turn off the heat and drop the piece of hot coal into the melted butter. It will begin to smoke. Cover the pan with a lid and leave the smoking coal to infuse the butter for 1 hour.

Stretch a muslin cloth over a sieve (wire mesh strainer). Strain the smoked butter through the lined sieve into a sterilized jar, discarding the coal. Store in the fridge and use as required for basting tikkas and kebabs.

Smoked Butter

CONDIMENTS

# SIDES & SALADS

What makes any tandoori sharing platter an absolute feast is definitely the side dishes. They play far more than a mere supporting role, they add texture, vibrancy and freshness to a meal with layers of flavour. I know that vegetables and salads can come across as an afterthought in Indian meals, but trust me, try these sides and you will understand how this chapter is bursting with so much goodness, from oven-roasted carrots that are glazed with mango chutney (Tandoori Chutneywalle Gajjar, page 160), a South Indian-style salad of green mango, carrots, cucumber and coconut (Kosumbari, page 164) to my family friend Deepa's recipe for a spiced orange salad with green chilli and coriander (Santre ka Salaad, page 168). These recipes are versatile and ought to be on every table alongside any chargrilled meats or vegetables.

# Broccoli, Cashew Nut & Coconut Stir Fry

## BROCCOLI PORIYAL

SERVES 4
AS A SIDE

'Poriyal' is a Tamil term for a stir fry or sautéed dish, and this cooking method works well with most leafy greens. I have used Tenderstem broccoli here for its wonderful colour and texture, stir fried with sliced red chilli, ginger matchsticks, coconut and curry leaves.

3 tbsp vegetable oil
handful of cashew nuts
1 tsp cumin seeds
2 heaped tsp black mustard
  seeds
½ tsp asafoetida (optional)
90 g (3¼ oz) halved and thinly
  sliced white onion
5 cm (2 in) ginger root, cut
  into matchsticks
12–15 curry leaves
1 mild red chilli, thinly sliced
350 g (12½ oz) Tenderstem
  broccoli, trimmed and halved
salt, to taste
2 tbsp grated (shredded)
  fresh coconut

Heat 1 tablespoon of the oil in a large wok or frying pan (skillet) over a medium heat. Add the cashew nuts and fry for 3–4 minutes. Drain in a bowl and set aside.

Add the remaining oil to the wok and, once hot, add the cumin seeds and mustard seeds. As they begin to splutter, add the asafoetida, if using, and sliced onions and fry for 6–7 minutes, stirring continuously. Add the ginger, curry leaves and red chilli and fry for 1 minute. Season to taste.

Add the broccoli to the wok and fry for 3 minutes. Add 100 ml (3½ fl oz/scant ½ cup) of water, reduce the heat to low, cover with a lid and cook for 7–8 minutes. Next, add the reserved cashew nuts and grated (shredded) coconut, stirring well, let everything mingle for 2 minutes.

Serve warm.

154

SIDES & SALADS

# Sweetcorn Stir Fry with Green Chilli, Ginger & Turmeric

## INDORE BHUTTE KI KEES

SERVES 4
AS A SIDE

Hailing from the city of Indore, this sweetcorn stir fry with green chilli, ginger and spices is a local favourite and served across streetfood stalls. If you prefer to make this vegan, opt for almond milk instead of dairy milk. Finishing the kees with chaat masala gives it the required tangy flavour that is characteristic of this dish.

740 g (1 lb 10 oz) canned sweetcorn, drained
3 tbsp vegetable oil
2 tsp black mustard seeds
½ tsp cumin seeds
pinch of asafoetida
5 cm (2 in) ginger root, grated (shredded)
2 green bird's-eye chillies, finely chopped
1 tsp ground turmeric
¼ tsp Kashmiri chilli powder (or mild chilli powder)
100 ml (3½ fl oz/scant ½ cup) whole (full-fat) milk
salt, to taste
1 tsp chaat masala
handful coriander (cilantro) leaves, finely chopped
handful grated (shredded) fresh coconut

Set aside a handful of the sweetcorn kernels and then blitz the rest to a coarse mixture in a blender.

Heat the oil in a non-stick saucepan over a medium heat. Add the mustard seeds and cumin seeds and, as they begin to splutter, add the asafoetida. Add ginger and green chillies and fry for 1 minute. Next, add the blended sweetcorn to the pan along with the turmeric and chill powder and fry for 5 minutes.

Reduce the heat to low, pour in the milk, season to taste and simmer with a lid on for 5 minutes, stirring halfway through the cooking time. Turn off the heat, add the chaat masala, chopped coriander (cilantro) and grated (shredded) coconut. Stir through the reserved whole sweetcorn kernels and season to taste.

Serve warm as a side with kebabs and roti.

# Chargrilled Green Beans with Roasted Peanuts, Sesame Seeds, Chilli & Lemon

## SHENGDANA BEANSCHI BHAJI

Green beans charred and topped with roasted peanuts, sesame seeds, chilli and burnt garlic. At my home in Mumbai, cooking green beans with peanuts was always a favourite and a classic recipe within the Maharashtrian community. My base recipe is something my mother made as a 'gawar ani shengdanyachi bhaji'; stir-fried veg, including local green beans, with crushed peanuts. I loved the idea of making it into a grilled salad that is so versatile and fresh. You can prepare this recipe in advance and warm it through just before serving. For years, I have served this as part of many home-cooked meals and even as a side for Christmas lunch. I have been asked many times for the recipe, so here it is at last!

2 tbsp white sesame seeds

600 g (1 lb 5 oz) green beans, trimmed

3 tbsp vegetable oil

6 garlic cloves, thinly sliced

3 tbsp salted roasted peanuts, coarsely crushed

2 tbsp coriander seeds, coarsely crushed

½ tsp Kashmiri chilli powder

2 tbsp roughly chopped coriander (cilantro) leaves

zest and juice of 1 lemon

Warm a large, dry frying pan (skillet) over a medium heat. Add the sesame seeds and toast for 1–2 minutes, shaking the pan often. Tip the toasted sesame seeds onto a plate and set aside.

Turn up the heat to high. Working in batches, if necessary, add the green beans to the same pan and cook for 7–8 minutes until they begin to colour and char slightly. Transfer the charred green beans to a plate and set aside.

Lower the heat to medium. Heat the oil in the pan, add the garlic and fry for 20 seconds. Return the green beans to the pan, stir well and add the crushed peanuts, coriander seeds, chilli powder and the toasted sesame seeds. Reduce the heat to low and cook, stirring, for 2–3 minutes. Season to taste. Turn off the heat, add the lemon zest and juice.

Serve the green beans warm with the chopped coriander (cilantro) scatted over the top.

# Roasted Carrots Glazed with Chilli–Mango Chutney

## TANDOORI CHUTNEYWALLE GAJJAR

I occasionally add shop-bought mango chutney to my curries, so I always keep a jar or two at home for adding that extra sweetness to dishes like these roasted carrots. There is something about lightly charred, roasted veg that perfectly soaks up any flavours you add. This marinade is simple, quick and creates deliciously sticky glazed carrots. Topped with crushed pistachios and fresh coriander (cilantro), it's a great side dish to serve as part of any Indian feast.

5 tbsp shop-bought
   mango chutney
zest and juice of 1 lime
1 tsp chilli flakes
2 tbsp vegetable oil
600 g (1 lb 5 oz) small carrots,
   peeled but with green tops left
   on and halved
handful of lightly roasted
   unsalted pistachios, crushed
handful of fresh coriander
   (cilantro) leaves, finely
   chopped
salt, to taste

Preheat the oven to 200°C fan (425°F/gas 7).

In a bowl, combine the mango chutney, lime zest and juice, chilli flakes, 1 tablespoon of the oil and pinch of salt. Mix well to make the glaze.

Put the carrots in a roasting dish. Set aside 1 tablespoon of the chilli-mango chutney glaze for later, then spread the rest of the glaze over the carrots.

Roast the carrots in the oven for 45 minutes. Halfway through the cooking time, stir and drizzle the remaining oil over the carrots, making sure they are well coated and cooking evenly.

Once the carrots are cooked through, mix the crushed pistachios into the reserved mango chutney glaze and drizzle over the carrots. Garnish the chutneywalle gajjar with the chopped coriander (cilantro) leaves and serve while warm.

# Red Onion, Tomato & Tamarind Chutney

## AWADH IMLIWALI PYAZ

I have enjoyed eating my way through many home-cooked meals in Lucknow, which were always accompanied by this delicious side dish. A tamarind spiced chutney that is soupy and thin is mixed with coriander (cilantro) and cracked black pepper, onions and tomatoes steeped in this mixture. For the longest time, I have wanted to include this recipe in one of my books! A refreshing side dish that is so good served with naan, pulao and grilled meats.

3 tbsp tamarind paste (check the strength and adjust to taste)

3 tsp caster (superfine) sugar

70 g (2½ oz) halved and thinly sliced red onion, mixed with a pinch of salt

70 g (2½ oz) halved and thinly sliced tomatoes

½ tsp Kashmiri chilli powder

1 tsp ground coriander

1 tsp coarsely crushed black peppercorns

2 tbsp finely chopped fresh coriander (cilantro)

### For the tempering

2 tbsp vegetable oil

1 tsp cumin seeds

2 dried mild red chillies

3 garlic cloves, finely chopped

10 curry leaves

Combine the tamarind paste and sugar in a mixing bowl with 250 ml (8½ fl oz/1 cup) of water. Stir well until all the sugar has dissolved. Add the sliced onions, tomatoes, chilli powder, ground coriander, crushed black peppercorns and fresh coriander (cilantro). Set aside while you make the tempering.

To make the tempering, heat the oil in a saucepan over a medium heat. Add the cumin seeds and dried chillies, then add the garlic and fry for 1 minute. Next, add the curry leaves and let them splutter for a few seconds.

Add the tamarind onion mixture to the pan with the tempering. Simmer over a low heat for 5 minutes. Turn off the heat and leave to cool before serving.

This chutney is perfect served with kebabs or tikkas.

# South Indian–Style Green Mango, Carrot & Cucumber Salad

## KOSUMBARI

A South Indian-style salad with green mango, carrots, cucumber and fresh coconut, finished with lots of lime and a spiced tempering, which gives it so much flavour. A green variety of mango is best for this recipe as it holds its shape while grating (shredding). I sometimes add a handful of mixed sprouts to this dish for a lovely texture.

250 g (9 oz) unripe raw mango (a green variety is best), peeled and coarsely grated (shredded)
100 g (3½ oz) carrots, peeled and grated (shredded)
200 g (7 oz) cucumber, peeled and finely chopped
100 g (3½ oz) grated (shredded) fresh coconut (frozen is fine too)
3 tbsp fresh coriander (cilantro) leaves, finely chopped
2 tsp sugar
juice of 2 limes
salt, to taste

### For the tempering

3 tbsp vegetable or coconut oil
1 tsp black mustard seeds
1 green bird's-eye chilli, finely chopped
10 curry leaves

Place the mango, carrots, cucumber and coconut in a large mixing bowl along with the chopped coriander (cilantro). Season generously with salt, then add the sugar and lime juice. Mix well.

To make the tempering, heat the oil in a small frying pan (skillet) over a medium heat. Add the mustard seeds and, as they begin to splutter, turn the heat off and quickly add the chilli and curry leaves.

Pour the tempering over the kosumbari in the bowl. Stir well to combine and then arrange the salad over a large platter before serving.

# Tangy Cucumber & Tomato Salad

## KACHUMBER

When thinking of Indian salads, most often they are narrowed down to a kachumber. As much as it's an obvious one, for me, a good kachumber is definitely a perfect salad, served on a sharing platter in the middle of the table for everyone to tuck in. My recipe is a rainbow salad with a colourful mix of cucumber, tomato, red onion, lime juice and fresh coriander (cilantro).

400 g (14 oz) cucumber, diced into bite-size pieces

200 g (7 oz) tomatoes, diced into bite-size pieces

100 g (3½ oz) red onion, thinly sliced

100 g (3½ oz) carrot, coarsely grated (shredded)

4 tbsp finely chopped fresh coriander (cilantro)

juice of 1 large lemon

1 tsp coarsely crushed cumin seeds

½ tsp Kashmiri chilli powder

1½ tbsp caster (superfine) sugar

salt, to taste

In a large mixing bowl, combine the diced cucumber and tomatoes, sliced red onion and grated (shredded) carrots along with the coriander (cilantro). Set aside.

In a small bowl, mix together the lemon juice, cumin seeds, chilli powder, sugar and salt. Stir well until the sugar has dissolved.

An hour before serving, pour the lemon dressing over the kachumber in the large mixing bowl. Mix well and leave at room temperature so that all the ingredients soak up the flavours of the dressing.

Arrange the kachumber over a large platter before serving.

# Spiced Cabbage Salad with Chilli, Curry Leaves, Turmeric & Lime

## GUJARATI SAMBHARO

A spiced cabbage salad from the west of India that is served as part of many Gujarati meals. Using cabbage, carrots and bell pepper flavoured with turmeric, chilli and lemon juice, this simple-to-prepare salad is brilliant for feeding a large crowd. Make this salad a few hours in advance so the vegetables have enough time to soak up the flavours of the spices.

500 g (1 lb 2 oz) white cabbage, thinly sliced

110 g (3¾ oz) carrots, peeled and coarsely grated (shredded)

1 medium red bell pepper, deseeded and sliced into thin strips

2 tbsp ghee

2 tsp black mustard seeds

pinch of asafoetida

2 green bird's-eye chillies, slit lengthwise

10 curry leaves

1 tsp ground coriander

½ tsp ground turmeric

1 tsp caster (superfine) sugar

juice of ½ lime

fresh coriander (cilantro) leaves, to garnish

salt, to taste

Place the sliced cabbage in a large mixing bowl and season well with salt. Cover the bowl with cling film (plastic wrap) and set aside for 30 minutes — the salt will draw out any excess moisture and the cabbage will soften.

Using kitchen paper, dab away any moisture from the bowl. Add the grated (shredded) carrots and red bell pepper strips to the cabbage in the bowl.

Heat the ghee in a heavy-based wok or *kadhai* over a medium flame. Add the mustard seeds and, as they begin to splutter, add the asafoetida, green chillies and curry leaves. Stir well and add the ground coriander and turmeric. Next, gradually add the vegetables, a little at a time, stirring well to make sure that everything is evenly coated in the flavoured oil. Cook for 2 minutes, stirring continuously.

Lower the heat, check the seasoning and add a little more salt only if necessary. Add the sugar and stir well. Cover and cook over a low heat for 4 minutes. Turn off the heat, add the lime juice and coriander (cilantro) leaves. Mix well.

Serve warm with rotis and kebabs.

# Spiced Orange Salad with Green Chilli & Coriander

SERVES 4
AS A SIDE

## SANTRE KA SALAAD

Our family friend Deepa Bisht, who hails from the region of Uttarakhand, makes the most delicious spiced orange salad when we get together for dinners. I wanted to include oranges in this chapter because they bring something unique to salads and sauces. This simple spiced orange salad is marinated with mild green chillies, crushed cumin seeds and fresh coriander (cilantro). The juice from the oranges lends the required sauciness and is great when serving breads and grilled food that needs a little something.

2 fat green chillies, finely chopped (you can use fewer if yours are spicy)
2 tsp dried red chilli flakes
1 tsp cumin seeds, coarsely crushed
3 tbsp white wine vinegar
2 tbsp caster (superfine) sugar
1 tsp black salt
8 large oranges, peeled and diced into bite-size pieces
2 spring onions (scallions), thinly sliced
2 tbsp coriander (cilantro) leaves, finely chopped
salt, to taste

Combine the chopped green chillies, chilli flakes, cumin seeds, vinegar, sugar and black salt in a small mixing bowl. Stir well until the sugar has dissolved. Set aside for 1 hour to allow the chillies to pickle and soften.

Place the oranges in a large bowl along with the spring onions (scallions). Pour over the dressing with the green chillies, then finish by scattering over the chopped coriander (cilantro). Season carefully to taste.

You can make this salad up to a day in advance as the oranges soak up all the spiced juices and marinate in the pickled green chillies.

168    SIDES & SALADS

# Apple, Beetroot & Mooli Salad

## SEB AUR CHUKANDAR KA SALAAD

Apple is commonly used in salads across India and in this recipe — one of my all-time favourites — it's combined with mooli (white or pink radish) and beetroot, then dressed with a mixture of lime juice, sugar and ground spices. The sweet, sour and tangy flavours and vibrant red colour make this the perfect salad to stuff in naan or serve alongside grilled meats or veggie kebabs.

300 g (10½ oz) Pink Lady apples, cut into matchsticks
250 g (8¾ oz) cooked beetroot (beets), cut into matchsticks or thin slices
300 g (10½ oz) mooli (white or pink radish), cut into matchsticks
2 tbsp finely chopped fresh coriander (cilantro) leaves
2 tbsp finely chopped fresh dill

### For the dressing
juice of 2 limes
3 tbsp caster (superfine) sugar
1½ tsp chaat masala
1 tsp Kashmiri chilli powder (or mild chilli powder)
1 tsp black salt

Place the apple, beetroot (beets) and mooli (radish) in a large mixing bowl and add the chopped coriander (cilantro) and dill.

In a separate small bowl, combine the lime juice with the sugar. Stir well until all the sugar has dissolved. Stir in the ground spices and black salt until everything is well combined.

An hour before serving, pour the lime dressing over the salad in the large mixing bowl. Toss to combine and leave at room temperature so that all the ingredients soak up the flavours of the dressing.

Arrange the salad over a large platter before serving.

# DESSERTS

Indians love something sweet — a 'meetha' — after a meal.
I'm definitely on board with that! In this chapter, I'm sharing some
of the best-loved Indian desserts that are all firm favourites during
the sweltering heat, like the Mango and Pistachio Kulfi (page 183).
My childhood favourite, the Fresh Fruit Cassata (page 184), never fails
to bring back many fond food memories. For something simple,
the Tandoori Phal (page 178), skewers of caramelized fruit with
white chocolate and cardamom cream, is always a crowd pleaser.

# Creamy Mango Yoghurt with Cardamom & Saffron

## AAMRAKHAND

A Maharashtrian dessert known as 'shrikhand' forms the base of this recipe. Shrikhand is a traditional dessert made with strained yoghurt and saffron. This delicious version, similar to a mango fool, is laced with sweetened mango purée and cardamom as well as saffron. If your mango purée isn't sweet enough, add a little extra sugar to sweeten the aamrakhand.

600 g (1 lb 5 oz) Greek yoghurt
300 ml (10 fl oz/1¼ cups) canned mango pulp
100 g (3½ oz/½ cup) caster (superfine) sugar
1 tsp green cardamom powder
pinch of saffron strands

### To serve

handful of crushed pistachios and almonds
100 g (3½ oz/½ cup) chopped fresh mango

Put the yoghurt into a piece of clean muslin. Gather up the edges of the muslin and tie them in a knot to secure. Hang the muslin over a kitchen tap (faucet) and leave it there for at least 7–8 hours or overnight to allow the moisture to drain and the yoghurt to thicken.

Unwrap the strained yoghurt and put it in a large mixing bowl. Add the mango pulp, sugar, cardamom and saffron, stir well and chill in the fridge for at least 4–6 hours to allow these ingredients to flavour the yoghurt well. If you have time, do this a day ahead as the flavours will intensify and be improved the following day.

Serve in individual bowls topped with a little of the crushed pistachios and almonds and the chopped mango.

# Caramelized Fruit with White Chocolate & Cardamom Cream

## TANDOORI PHAL

Fresh fruit is such a revelation when grilled; the natural sugars in the fruit caramelize and take on a wonderful smoky flavour. Here a variety of fruits, including apples, peaches, pineapple and strawberries, is served up on skewers with a drizzle of white chocolate and cardamom-infused cream. If you have ever eaten the fruit cream found across cities in North India, well this is a grown-up version of that!

You will need wooden skewers soaked in cold water for 30 minutes

300 g (10½ oz) apples, cored
280 g (10 oz) peaches, pitted
280 g (10 oz) pineapple, peeled
 (I use canned)
250 g (8¾ oz) large
 strawberries, hulled

### For the chocolate cream

360 g (12¾ oz) white chocolate
160 ml (5½ fl oz/⅔ cup) double
 (heavy) cream
1 tsp ground green cardamom
handful of crushed pistachios

Dice all the fruit into bite-size pieces. Thread the fruit pieces onto the soaked wooden skewers, making sure there is a mixture of different fruits on each one.

To make the chocolate cream, melt the white chocolate in a heatproof bowl set over a pan of boiling water. Stir the cream and cardamom into the melted chocolate. Mix well and set aside.

Heat the griddle pan over a high heat.

Working in batches, cook the fruit skewers in the griddle pan for 8–9 minutes, turning them occasionally. Take them off the heat and transfer to a serving platter.

When ready to serve, drizzle over the chocolate cream and top with the crushed pistachios. Place the bowl of remaining chocolate cream on the table in case anyone wants to help themselves to some extra.

# No-Churn Rose & Cardamom Ice Cream

I don't own an ice-cream maker as I have no space in my kitchen to store one. It's probably the reason why I have always aimed to come up with a no-churn ice-cream recipe that really works. This cheat's ice cream is made with double (heavy) cream and condensed milk flavoured by green cardamom, rose water, dried rose petals and pistachios. Easy to mix, freeze and serve, and delicious to eat.

8 green cardamom pods (seeds only)
280 ml (9½ fl oz/1 cup plus 3 tbsp) double (heavy) cream
2 tbsp rose water
1 x 400 g (14 oz) can condensed milk
1 tbsp dried rose petals
20 g (¾ oz) pistachios, roughly chopped

Grind the green cardamom seeds in a pestle and mortar to a fine powder.

In a bowl, whisk the cream with the rose water and cardamom powder until soft peaks form. Next, lightly fold the condensed milk, dried rose petals and most of the crushed pistachios into the whipped cream.

Transfer the ice-cream mixture into a freezerproof, airtight container. Scatter the remaining pistachios over the top of the ice cream and place in the freezer for 6–8 hours, or preferably overnight.

When ready to serve, let the ice cream stand at room temperature for 5–10 minutes to soften slightly, then scoop into individual bowls.

# Mango & Pistachio Kulfi

## MALAI KULFI

Malai kulfi eaten on a hot summer's day on the bustling street of Ajmer; to be honest, it was like nothing mattered except that stick of kulfi melting in the sweltering heat. Traditionally, kulfi is dense, flavoured evaporated milk pressed into metal cones and left to freeze in a mixture of ice and rock salt. I have added mango and pistachios to this simple recipe that replicates the taste of many childhood memories of eating malai kulfi.

You will need ice-lolly moulds
  and sticks

300 ml (10 fl oz/1¼ cups) double
  (heavy) cream
200 ml (6¾ fl oz/¾ cup) canned
  mango pulp
200 ml (6¾ fl oz/¾ cup)
  condensed milk
100 ml (3½ fl oz/scant ½ cup)
  evaporated milk
1 tsp ground green cardamom
generous handful of pistachios,
  finely chopped

In a large bowl, whisk the cream to soft peaks and set aside.

In a separate mixing bowl, combine the mango pulp, condensed milk, evaporated milk, cardamom and half the chopped pistachios. Add the whisked cream to this bowl and fold through making sure everything is well mixed and there are no lumps.

Divide the kulfi mixture equally between 8 ice-lolly moulds. Add the sticks and then place the ice-lolly moulds in the freezer for 7–8 hours.

When ready to serve, dip the moulds in hot water to release the kulfi lollies. Coat with the remaining chopped pistachios before serving.

# Fresh Fruit Cassata

For every '80s kid, cassata was the only reason to visit the Kwality ice-cream shop in Mumbai. I remember sitting in the shop eating a slice of this ice-cream cake on a paper plate, fully committed to my cassata. Before you go thinking this distant cousin had anything to do with the elegant Italian version, think again! This gaudy-coloured, three-tier ice-cream cake is packed with fresh and candied fruit and pistachios. Including this recipe here brings back nostalgic memories for me, and no doubt for other readers who can relate to this dessert, which has played such a big part for our generation.

200 g (7 oz) vanilla ice cream
200 g (7 oz) strawberry ice cream
200 g (7 oz) pistachio ice cream
280 g (10 oz) Madeira cake, cut
    into 4 cm (1½ in) thick slices
splash of dark rum (optional)
100 g (3½ oz) mixed candied fruit
handful of almonds and
    pistachios, roughly crushed
400 g (14 oz) fresh mango,
    peeled and finely chopped

Before you begin layering the cassata, take all three ice creams out of the freezer and leave to soften for 30 minutes.

Line a 900 g loaf tin (2 lb loaf pan) with cling film (plastic wrap). Leave the edges of the cling film overhanging the sides of the tin — you can use it later to lift the cassata out of the tin when unmoulding.

Lay the Madeira cake slices over the base of the loaf tin. Press down lightly to make sure all the corners of the tin are covered. Use any leftover cake to fill any gaps or line the sides of the tin. Drizzle over a few tablespoons of rum, if using, and let that soak into the cake.

Add scoops of the vanilla ice cream to the cake-lined tin. Using the back of a spoon, flatten the ice cream out into an even layer over the cake. Top with a thin layer of the candied fruit and a small amount of the crushed almonds and pistachios. Next, add the strawberry ice cream to the tin and again flatten it out slightly into an even layer. Cover the ice cream all over with a thin layer of the mango pieces. Now, add the pistachio ice cream to the tin, spreading it out evenly to make the final layer. Finish with the remaining crushed almonds and pistachios. Place in the freezer for at least 6 hours or overnight.

When ready to serve, take the cassata out of the freezer and leave to soften for 30 minutes. Using the cling film, lift the cassata out of the tin and onto a serving plate, then peel away the lining. Cut into thick slices and serve.

# DRINKS

Indian drinks round off any good meal and bring along a fun element too. Some recipes include spices — my favourite has got to be the spiced tamarind drink with mint, coriander, ginger and chilli (Jal Jeera, page 196). As much as Thandai (page 192), a chilled almond milk drink infused with fennel, cardamom and rose, is made during the festival of Holi, I also enjoy a boozy version during the festive season with a splash of gin or vodka.

DRINKS

# Ice-Cream Float with Jelly, Chia Seeds, Noodles & Crushed Pistachios

## FALOODA

A party in a glass is how I like to describe this ice-cream float! Growing up in India, I have enjoyed one too many faloodas. The best part is how they come in so many different flavours, from custard apple to mango and rose. A tall sundae glass is filled with fruit coulis, chia seeds (or sabza/basil seeds), fruit jelly, cold glass noodles, and scoops of ice cream. The glass is then topped up with chilled milk and garnished with chopped fresh fruit and crushed pistachios. So good!

30 g (1 oz) chia seeds
100 g (3½ oz) fine rice
   vermicelli noodles
220 ml (7½ fl oz) berry coulis
135 g (4¾ oz) strawberry jelly
   (jello), ready-made is fine
whole (full-fat) milk, chilled
vanilla ice cream
handful of fresh strawberries,
   roughly chopped
handful of crushed pistachios

Chill four tall glasses in the fridge while you prepare the ingredients for the falooda.

Soak the chia seeds in a bowl with plenty of water for 20 minutes. Scoop out the soaked chia seeds, discard the water and set aside.

Meanwhile, boil the noodles for 8–10 minutes. Drain and set aside.

When ready to assemble the falooda, lay out all the ingredients so that you can work quickly.

Pour 3–4 tablespoons of the berry coulis into the bottom of each chilled glass, followed by 2 teaspoons of the chia seeds and 3 tablespoons of the strawberry jelly (jello). Top with a handful of noodles.

Fill each glass with chilled milk to two-thirds of the way up and then add a generous scoop of vanilla ice cream. Garnish with the chopped strawberries crushed and pistachios.

# Chilled Almond Milk Infused with Fennel, Cardamom & Rose

THANDAI

Thandai is served during celebrations and consumed in copious quantities. It's a delicious addition to any meal. This recipe makes a generous amount of the almond milk drink, but as everyone will undoubtedly find it deliciously moreish, you will be glad of having enough for extra portions.

20 whole almonds
handful of cashew nuts
2 tbsp white poppy seeds
7–8 green cardamom pods
    (seeds only)
½ tsp fennel seeds
1 tbsp dried rose petals,
    plus a few extra to garnish
100 g (3½ oz/½ cup) caster
    (superfine) sugar
500 ml (17 fl oz/2⅛ cups) whole
    (full-fat) milk

Soak the almonds and cashew nuts together in a bowl in plenty of water. In a separate bowl, soak the poppy seeds in 100 ml (3½ fl oz/scant ½ cup) of water. Leave these both to soak for at least 3 hours.

Place the cardamom seeds, fennel seeds and rose petals in a spice grinder and grind to a coarse powder. Mix this powder with the sugar in a large mixing bowl.

Drain the soaked almonds and cashew nuts, discarding the water. Peel the skins from the almonds. Place the nuts in a blender along with the poppy seeds and their soaking water. Grind to a fine, smooth paste. (I use a NutriBullet for this.)

In a measuring jug (cup), combine the milk and the nut paste. Stir well, making sure all the paste has dissolved in the milk.

Pour this nut milk mixture through a fine sieve (mesh strainer) into the bowl of sugar and spices. Stir well and then top up with 200 ml (6¾ fl oz/¾ cup) of water. Decant into a large serving jug (pitcher) and chill in the fridge for a few hours.

Before serving, stir the thandai and pour into individual glasses and top with a few extra dried rose petals.

# Indian Spiced Lemonade

## BANTA SODA

If you are scouring the streets of Delhi for refreshment during the hot summer, there is a strong chance you will have come across this little beauty. It's very hard to miss the lemon-topped sealed glass bottles stacked on a street cart! Those bottles contain a local lemonade that's also known as Masala Banta Soda, which is made with Indian lemons, spices and fizzy water. Tangy, refreshing and utterly delicious! This is a recipe that is traditionally made with Indian lemons, however, as that variety of lemons is not widely available outside of India, I have swapped them here for limes to give the drink it's required sour flavour.

juice of 5 limes
3 tbsp caster (superfine) sugar
pinch of coarsely crushed
    black pepper
2 tsp black salt
1 tsp cumin seeds,
    coarsely crushed
2 x 500 ml (17 fl oz) bottles
    of Sprite
ice, to serve

In a large serving jug (pitcher), mix together the lime juice, sugar, black pepper, black salt and cumin. Stir well and then top up with the Sprite and add lots of ice. Serve chilled.

# Spiced Tamarind Drink with Mint, Coriander, Ginger & Chilli

## JAL JEERA

This is one of my favourite drinks, combining mint, coriander (cilantro), ginger and chilli. The addition of tamarind gives it its tangy flavour, which you can adjust to your taste by altering the quantity of paste used based on its strength. Served the drink chilled in a jug (pitcher) with lots of ice and a scattering of boondi. Boondi is a gram flour snack that is added to sweet and savoury dishes and works really well in this drink giving it texture. Jal Jeera freezes well too, so make a little extra ready for your next dinner with friends. Just defrost it, then served chilled and freshly garnished with boondi.

50 g (1¾ oz) coriander
  (cilantro) leaves
30 g (1 oz) mint leaves
1.5 cm (½ in) ginger root,
  roughly chopped
2 tbsp tamarind paste (check the
  strength and adjust to taste)
60 g (2 oz/¼ cup) caster
  (superfine) sugar
1 green bird's-eye chilli,
  slit lengthwise
boondi (a shop-bought snack
  made from chickpea/gram
  flour), to garnish

### For the spice mix
½ tsp cumin seeds
1 tsp black peppercorns
½ tsp fennel seeds
½ tsp black salt
½ tsp dried mango powder

Put all the spice mix ingredients in a pestle and mortar and crush to a powder.

Put the coriander (cilantro), mint, ginger and tamarind paste in a blender along with 60 ml (4 tablespoons) of water and blend to a smooth paste.

In a large serving jug (pitcher), combine this paste with the sugar and 1.2 litres (1¼ quarts/5 cups) of water. Mix well and add the spice mix. Stir well and add the green chilli. Chill in the fridge to allow the green chilli to infuse the jal jeera.

When ready to serve, stir well and pour into individual glasses. Top each glass with small spoonful of boondi.

# Sour Mango Slushie

## AAM KA GOLA

Sour mango, tart lime and warming ginger combine to make this Indian slushie so moreish. I guarantee you will want to make this drink all year round. I have added a splash of tequila but you can easily leave that out for a non-alcoholic version.

450 g (1 lb) fresh mango, peeled and cut into chunks
200 ml (6¾ fl oz/¾ cup) canned mango pulp
zest and juice of 2 limes
1 piece of stem ginger, finely chopped, plus 1 tbsp of the syrup from the jar
splash of tequila (optional)

Put the mango chunks, 150 ml (5½ fl oz/scant ⅔ cup) of the mango pulp and the lime juice in a blender and blitz to a purée. Transfer to a freezerproof container along with the chopped stem ginger. Stir well and freeze for 3–4 hours. You want some ice crystals to form but the mixture to still be slushy.

Take the aam ka gola out of the freezer and use a fork to scrape it into a rough mixture. Spoon into glasses or bowls and serve with a drizzle of the remaining mango pulp, the ginger syrup and a little lime zest. Add a splash of tequila, if you prefer an alcoholic version.

# MENU PLANS

For me, planning a dinner is always one the most exciting parts of having friends over. Indians thrive on sharing delicious meals, no matter how big or small the event. A lot of how we feel is relayed through the food we cook and ultimately share. Food becomes an extension of us; feeding family and friends is a way of conveying our unconditional love and warmth. It's something that generations of the women in my family have done, revelling in the joy of watching everyone savour the flavours. The feasts within this chapter of menu plans are a collection of recipes that are for every occasion. They are generous and perfect for a crowd. More than that, they are tailor-made for our lifestyle, offering variety and flavour with ease.

Vegetarian Feast

MENU PLANS

# MENU PLANS

## VEGETARIAN FEAST

One of the best parts of having friends over at the weekend is planning a vegetarian menu that everyone can tuck into and sample all the dishes on the table. My all-time favourites are the whole roasted cauliflower (Gobi Tandoori, page 94) and the sticky mango chutney glazed carrots (Tandoori Chutneywalle Gajjar, page 160), which everyone loves. Partner these crowd-pleasing vegetarian dishes with some tandoori roti, fresh salads and chutneys and you are on to a winner.

*See photo on pages 204–5.*

### Whole Roasted Cauliflower in a Creamy Coconut & Chilli Sauce
GOBI TANDOORI, PAGE 94

### Roasted Carrots Glazed with Chilli-Mango Chutney
ANDOORI CHUTNEYWALLE GAJJAR, PAGE 160

### Broccoli, Cashew Nut & Coconut Stir Fry
BROCCOLI PORIYAL, PAGE 154

### Spicy Coconut & Cashew Chutney
NARIYAL AUR KAJU KI CHUTNEY, PAGE 133

### Garlic & Ghee Naan
PAGE 110

## VEGAN FEAST

When planning Indian meals you inherently know there is such a variety of beautiful vegan dishes that it's easy to bring a select few together. If I'm honest, this might be my favourite of all the feasts shown here — it includes many of my favourite recipes. The chargrilled green beans with roasted peanuts and sesame seeds (page 158) are a revelation and not forgetting the Indore-style spiced sweetcorn (page 156) and double-marinated aubergine (eggplant) tikkas (page 89) — swap the whole milk yoghurt for plain vegan yoghurt where required. Serve a selection of breads, chutneys and pickles to bring texture, tang, freshness and flavour.

*See photo on pages 208–9.*

### Green Bell Peppers Stuffed with Spicy Potatoes, Chilli & Dried Mango

TANDOORI SHIMLA MIRCH, PAGE 96

### Aubergine Tikkas in Creamy Yoghurt, Mustard, Chilli & Ginger

TANDOORI BAINGAN, PAGE 89

### Sweetcorn Stir Fry with Green Chilli, Ginger & Turmeric

INDORE BHUTTE KI KEES, PAGE 156

### Chargrilled Green Beans with Roasted Peanuts, Sesame Seeds, Chilli & Lemon

SHENGDANA BEANSCHI BHAJI, PAGE 158

### Roasted Tomato Chutney

BHUNE TAMATAR KI CHUTNEY, PAGE 128

### Quick Tawa Roti

PAGE 115

## MEAT FEAST

When you think of Indian tikkas and kebabs, the repertoire is always focused on the meat. When planning a feast that includes meat, I want to showcase chicken and lamb alongside dishes with different textures. For me, nothing beats a classic tandoori chicken tikka, and once you have tried my recipe (page 24) you will know it's anything but basic. The double-marination technique gives it the required texture and keeps the chicken moist. Also the inclusion of Tawe ka Tikka (page 54) on the table brings back the nostalgia of Lawrence Road and not forgetting the crowd-pleasing Shami Kebabs (page 59).

*See photo on pages 210–11.*

### Tandoori Chicken Tikka

PAGE 24

### Stir-Fried Lamb with Garlic, Green Chilli & Garam Masala

TAWE KA TIKKA, PAGE 54

### Lamb Kebabs with Cardamom, Chilli & Mint

SHAMI KEBABS, PAGE 59

### Spicy Green Chilli Chutney

HARI MIRCH KI CHUTNEY, PAGE 136

### Spiced Flatbreads with Kashmiri Chilli & Carom Seeds

KHAMIRI ROTI, PAGE 116

### Spiced Tamarind Drink with Mint, Coriander, Ginger & Chilli

JAL JEERA, PAGE 196

Meat Feast

## T

# Acknowledgements

**JOHANN**  For being my constant cheerleader and tasting every single recipe in this book with joy and enthusiasm. You bring colour to everything I do.

**BHARAT**  I am so grateful for the life we live and your unwavering support. I'm happiest when I'm cooking the meals you love, enjoying our food-filled adventures and faking my occasional interest in T20 cricket! I love you.

**HOLLY**  Thank you always for your advice and continued support. I hope you know how much I appreciate what you do for me, making magic happen and keeping me right through this ride. Here's to many more delicious meals with cocktails.

**KAJAL**  My brilliant publishing director, thank you for putting together Team THC, for your kindness and tenacity, and for giving my ideas a platform. More than anything, thank you for affording me the privilege of writing cookbooks.

**EMMA**  For steering this book through the months of discussions, writing and shooting. Thank you for listening to me talk about Indian food, for your words of reassurance in every meeting, and for sharing in my excitement in it all.

As much as my name is on the cover, this book has been such a collaborative project with a collective pool of talent that continually makes me feel so lucky to have the opportunity to work with you all.

**LISA**  Thank you for being the voice in my head, reasoning, discussing and navigating the spine of my work. Writing can be such an isolating process, but to you have oversee *Tandoori Home Cooking* has given me confidence in what I have put down on paper — it's hugely appreciated.

**EILA**  Your patience, guidance and advice have been so vital over the last few months. I could not have asked for more.

**ISSY**  You have made the food in this book look delicious! Being on a shoot with you and watching you effortlessly bring to life my work each day has been a joy and most definitely emotional. Thank you for your patience, listening to me chat about spices, cooking and sharing in our mutual love for India.

**EMILY**  Such a full circle moment for us from the time you supported me while filming with Jamie Oliver years ago and to now elegantly styling the dishes on the pages of *Tandoori Home Cooking*. I am grateful to have worked with you; your warmth, ease and always being a ray of sunshine have made me feel like I belonged. I cannot wait to travel across India with you.

Thank you to Emily's marvellous team Hugo, Clare, Joe, Jordan, Anna and Isabel, not least for listening to me all day, every day constantly say 'Read the recipe!'

**EVI AND HER TEAM**   I feel a cookbook is only as good as it looks and you have brought my food to life in *Tandoori Home Cooking*.

**BECKY AND LAURA**   I have had the privilege of working closely with you both and have always been in awe of your dedication and drive. It's been so much fun and I genuinely thrive in the process of getting my book out to the world because I have you wonderful ladies supporting me throughout.

## To my Mumbai team...

**PANKAJ**   You amazing, wonderful man. Your brilliance is in capturing the essence of our city in every frame. And to Dwij for making those shoot days easy, fun, and keeping the wonderful vegetable vendors happy.

**MEGHNA**   I feel so lucky to have had you as part of this shoot. You are such a talent, but more than that spending hours chatting about food, recipes and cooking was the best. And to Jeena for all her support.

**PRIYANKA**   Pri, you bring joy, happiness and good vibes to every room you are in. I know this shoot was the most fun because you agreed to join me. Thank you for being my shadow and helping me own each frame.

A lot of my work over the past two decades has been about celebrating regional Indian cooking and has been at the heart of what I do. To watch a shift in perception and how this wonderful cuisine is being embraced over the last few years has been a moment, a movement and an opportunity to keep that wave of enthusiasm going. I will continue to champion food from my community not only to get the word out there but for people of every generation to understand more about Indian cuisine, cooking techniques, spices and communities. It's a privilege and a platform I do not take for granted and I have you all, my readers, to thank for the kind messages, unwavering support and love that you bring to me daily. Thank you for sharing the joy of Indian cooking through my cookbooks and more importantly cooking these dishes in your homes.

# About the Author

Maunika Gowardhan (aka @cookinacurry) is an Indian chef and bestselling author, with a career that stems from her love for authentic flavours, cooking techniques and being able to share a fresh perspective on the cuisine.

Through her work in food she creates and shares traditional Indian dishes with exciting flavours and ingredients that are reflective of her heritage and upbringing in Mumbai. Her approach to cooking is simple and enticing with the use of earthy spices, fresh herbs and blends that are synonymous with India, based around dishes that are accessible and recipes that are cooked from communities across India; many of which have been part of her own family for generations.

Maunika is a popular contributor to titles including *Good Housekeeping*, *olive magazine*, *BBC Food* and BBC 1's *Morning Live*, and is the contributing editor for *Vogue India* often writing about the London food scene. *Tandoori Home Cooking* is her third cookbook; her much-anticipated second book, *Thali* became a Times bestseller, and followed her internationally loved debut cookbook, *Indian Kitchen*.

Published in 2023 by Hardie Grant Books,
an imprint of Hardie Grant Publishing

Hardie Grant Books (London)
5th & 6th Floors
52–54 Southwark Street
London SE1 1UN

Hardie Grant Books (Melbourne)
Building 1, 658 Church Street
Richmond, Victoria 3121

hardiegrantbooks.com

British Library Cataloguing-in-Publication Data. A catalogue record
for this book is available from the British Library.

Tandoori Home Cooking
ISBN: 978-1-78488-578-6

10 9 8 7 6 5 4 3 2

Publishing Director: Kajal Mistry
Acting Publishing Director: Emma Hopkin
Design: Evi-O Studio | Evi O., Susan Le, Emi Chiba & Katherine Zhang
Photographer: Issy Croker
Food and Props Stylist: Emily Ezekiel
Project Editor: Lisa Pendreigh
Proofreader: Jo Ireson
Indexer: Vanessa Bird
Production Controller: Gary Hayes

Colour reproduction by p2d
Printed and bound in China by Leo Paper Products Ltd.